How to Train Your Own
GUN DOG

by CHARLES S. GOODALL

Second Edition—First Printing

1988

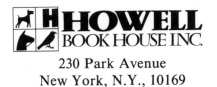

HOWELL
BOOK HOUSE INC.

230 Park Avenue
New York, N.Y., 10169

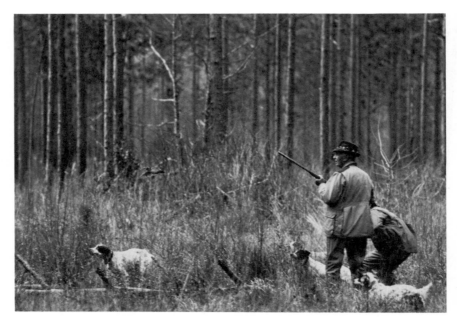

John T. Pirie, Jr., former president and chairman of the board of Carson, Pirie, Scott & Co., is an enthusiastic outdoorsman. Here he is walking up to flush a Carolina quail for his English Setter. A Setter brace mate backs staunchly while a young Pointer is pushed forward and stroked to further insure the trainee learns to back well. *Outdoor Life*

Library of Congress Cataloging-in-Publication Data

Goodall, Charles S.
   How to train your own gun dog / by Charles S. Goodall. 2nd ed.
     p. cm.
   ISBN 0-87605-562-5
   1. Hunting dogs—Training. I. Title.
SF428.5.G66   1988   87-36661
636.7'52—dc19

Credits

It is physically impossible to acknowledge the pictures, ideas and factual data contributed by scores of gun dog owners from all sections of the country. But it would be manifestly unfair to omit the names of those who contributed so much of their time and effort to make this book possible. The author does gratefully acknowledge the contributions of the following:

Andy Shoaff, of J. A. Shoaff and Associates, Newport Beach, California, for the superb photography of the sequence training routine illustrations for Pointing Dogs and Spaniels. His excellent photography was spread over a dozen locations in California, Illinois and Wisconsin. If his gun dogs are as excellent as his photography, he will have a kennelful of National Champions.

My wife, Zelda M. Goodall, for typing the manuscript and proof reading the finished copy, when she would rather have been playing golf or bridge, or painting new "old masters."

—Chuck Goodall

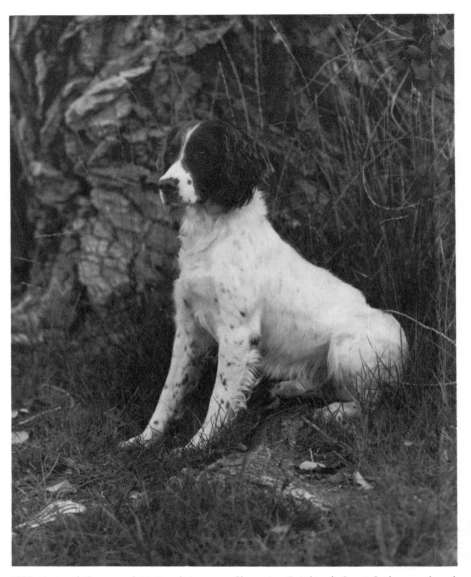

1983 National Open and National Amateur Champion Saighton's Scout 2nd, owned and handled by Jess Sekey of Colorado. Scout has also won Field Champion and Amateur Field Champion titles before his great wins in the 1983 Nationals. This great Springer was sired by another great one—Dr. Janet Christensen's Quadruple National Champion Saighton's Scud.

Contents

About the Author

CHARLES S. (CHUCK) GOODALL IS ONE of Nature's noblemen, a superb hunter with an unrivalled background in gun dogs, including the pointing breeds, spaniels and retrievers. Chuck Goodall has been a hunter and amateur trainer of gun dogs for more than forty years. He grew up in Southern Illinois and dates his addiction to upland game and waterfowl hunting with dogs from his early youth. He confesses he was frequently in trouble with school authorities who had the temerity to schedule classes on opening day of quail, pheasant, duck and dove seasons.

Chuck Goodall's dedication to good dog work stems from the fact that early-on he became convinced that 95% of the excitement and appeal of hunting came from observing the actions of home-trained pointing dogs, spaniels or retrievers in finding and retrieving game.

Goodall became interested in field trials when he witnessed several American Field Futurities held near his Southern Illinois home in the 1930s. After graduation from the University of Illinois he found that field trials enabled him to utilize and enjoy spending time with his dogs in the field for eight or ten months each year instead of just during the ever-decreasing open hunting seasons.

It's evident that he was a successful amateur trainer because he placed home-trained dogs in field trials more than 150 times! He has also served as a field trial judge for the several breeds in sixteen states on more than one hundred occasions. Many hunting trips to a dozen or more states, Mexico and Canada helped to broaden his knowledge of canine behavior as well as that of many species of upland game and waterfowl.

His experience embraces distinguished service as a club official, as a lecturer for sportsmen's clubs, and a reporter of significant trials. Indeed, Chuck Goodall is one of America's outstanding authorities on hunting dogs and field trials, uniquely equipped to author this excellent book. He is preeminently qualified to tell others how to train their gun dogs.

—William F. Brown
Editor, *The American Field*

Mr. Brown's foregoing remarks speak volumes for the kind of person, hunter and contributor Charles Goodall is to the whole area of hunting game with dogs. His credentials are impressive and the honors that have been bestowed upon him over the years have been truly well-deserved.

Notable among these honors was the first Martin Hogan Memorial Award (1952) for the individual who contributed most to gun dogs and the sport of field trials in the Middle West.

A partial list of the organizations he served and the capacities he served in is singularly impressive. He was a member of the Board of Trustees of the Morris Animal Foundation from 1967 to 1977 and served as Chairman of the Canine Division for four years. He was a Governor of the English Springer Spaniel Field Trial Association for 27 years and Secretary of the English Springer Spaniel Field Trial Club of Illinois for 28 years. Additionally, he was a founder and officer of the Illinois River Retriever Club and the Secretary of the North Arkansas Bird Dog Club for six years.

A prolific writer, Mr. Goodall is the author of three other books on gun dog training and over two hundred articles and stories on gun dogs and related subjects. It is evident that the gun dog fraternity would have been far poorer without Charles Goodall's long, devoted service to it.

Here now is a new book that will be read, enjoyed and utilized by thousands of outdoorsmen who value a well trained dog. May your reading result in a top-drawer hunting companion and many full game bags for a long time to come.

—The Publisher

Introduction

THE CAREFULLY-DETAILED, step-by-step training routines described in this book are presented to help novice and experienced dog owners avoid the pitfalls and disappointments of hunting with what might be called "spot trained" dogs. For instance, a pointing dog which has been taught only to hold point staunchly by the electric training collar, or by an ounce of birdshot in his rear end, can cause his owner much pain in a hundred different ways. Chasing livestock, killing chickens, getting lost, or becoming gun shy are a few examples. If not taken in hand before such undesirable behavior patterns become fixed habits, the dog may become incorrigible. The spaniel which punches out 75 or more yards while questing, or chases every airborne bird including field larks, won't put much meat in his owner's game bag. And the retriever which has not been educated to sit quietly in a blind, can flare most of the game which was headed in the hunter's direction. Owners of half-trained gun dogs will often remark, "Well, Spot blew a few (?) today, but he sure hunted hard and will improve with age." But the truth is he won't improve unless a miracle occurs, and he may get worse. His actions, like Alex Karas' pro football linemen who "hold just a little bit," are deliberate, and his usefulness as a gun dog is nil.

We urge you, the owner, to ignore the advice of the one who says the only way to train a dog is to take him hunting, because it "tain't" so. Do take him hunting, of course. That is the only way to develop a top gun dog. But do give him some schooling first in daily ten-minute sessions in the yard and longer ones in the field with planted birds and repetitious training routines. The one hundred hours spent in yard and field training during the dog's first eighteen months will condition him to perform correctly with manners and class. You will both have more fun and more productive hunting for the next seven or eight years of Spot's active life. But do go as an observer or Puppy Stake contender to a field trial for your breed (locations and dates listed in publications found in Bibliography). You will be amazed by the high degree of training a dog can absorb and by the controlled spontaneity and eager desire the older dogs will exhibit while performing before the gun.

The second edition of this book will outline training procedures with photographic illustrations for pointing dogs, flushing spaniels and retrievers. The section on spaniels may be used by owners of retrievers and other flushing breeds to train other non-pointing breeds to work before the gun. The section on retrievers may be used for training any dog to become a good water worker and blind retriever.

We have included counts and harvest totals of waterfowl and migratory game birds in each of the four great flyways. New chapters will describe how to hunt the several species of game birds and waterfowl with the correct pointing or flushing dog. We allow that some suggestions as to the correct dog will be controversial since gun dog owners may have some breed loyalty and certain individuals within a breed often have a special aptitude for particular species of game.

A gun dog worthy of the name must be able to perform willingly, obediently and productively in the traditional, typical style of the breed. The ability to do so is based on three factors; field-bred ancestors, thorough training in the yard or field and considerable experience in the field on wild game. There is no substitute for any of these important conditions. The absence of any one may eliminate the animal as an acceptable hunting dog.

Game birds are found in quantity only in those areas where there is ample food and cover. The good hunting dog, especially in the pointing breeds, can only learn to handle different birds if he is worked on each type a half dozen times or more. When hunted in soybean or corn country, the young prospect will soon learn that pheasant and Bobwhite Quail like edges and often can be found in stubble fields, fence rows or wood lots. In prairie hunting where stock grazing is the principal agricultural activity, the sagacious prospect soon learns that game will usually be found in cover, since their normal food supply will be seeds from native grasses and weeds. In timber, where there are Grouse and Woodcock, the dog learns through instinct or training that he must keep track of his handler and will often shorten his range to fit the terrain.

The flushing dog also needs experience in a variety of cover and terrain to learn how to handle moving game. However, since this is a beater who must remain within gunshot range, the quartering pattern he has learned from training will vary little from one type of cover to another. The flushing dog, in most cases, has a special aptitude for retrieving waterfowl from a blind or pass shoot, conditions seldom encountered with pointing dogs. The flusher is also highly useful for jump shooting in marshy wetlands, in front of a walking hunter or one cruising the shoreline in a boat. Such hunting requires a strong, well-conditioned dog such as a retriever, but the Springer Spaniel can perform well too, if in hard running condition.

The hunting routines suggested in this book were learned and developed by the author from forty years of experience with his own dogs. It is not possible to train a gun dog by reading a book. However, learning how others have successfully developed and trained good gun dogs can be helpful. We hope this becomes a well-thumbed volume.

Dan Langhans, who, with many of his trainees, modeled many of the training sequences in this book, began with gun dogs as an amateur trainer-handler. He trained his great, homebred Springer, Dansmirth Gunshot and won both the National Amateur and the National Open in 1969. Langhans subsequently turned professional and continues in training gun dogs for others.

Glossary of Hunting Dog Terminology

JUST AS PRACTICALLY every leisure activity has its own particular language, so too does the sport of hunting with dogs. The jargon of the gunner is especially colorful, adding its own special dimension to the entire pastime. You will find the language of the field used throughout this book and the following list of terms with their meanings is given here so you can better understand what is being presented before and as you train your dog.

Applicable to All Gun Dogs

Back Casting: Searching for game behind the hunter instead of to the front.

Backing: Staunchly pointing another dog which is pointing game.

Blinker: A dog which avoids game he knows is present or refuses to handle it; a serious fault.

Bolter: A dog which ignores its handler and goes off to hunt on its own.

Cast: The distance or range a dog extends his hunting pattern while questing for game.

Cover: Grass, weeds or cultivated crops in a hunting area.

Covey Rise: The unified flight of quail or other game birds which normally flush together as a unit.

Hard Buck: A twelve-inch piece of wood encircled by a metal sleeve to which bird wings have been attached.

Hard Mouth: A serious fault in which a dog chews or damages game while retrieving.

Honoring: Same as Backing. See.

Making Game: The animation and excitement displayed by a dog to indicate that game is near.

Marking a Fall: The ability to go to the exact spot where shot game fell.

Potter: Lingering with and reworking game scent unproductively.

Objectives: Places where game is likely to be found; corners of pastures, hedgerows, etc.

Runner: Game which moves ahead of the questing dog or a wing tipped cripple which can run but not fly.

Steady to Wing and Shot: The action of a dog trained to remain at the spot game is flushed and shot until ordered to retrieve or resume hunting.

Style Up: Adjusting the position of a pointing dog (especially raising head and tail) to achieve a more attractive point.

Wild Flush: Birds which lift or flush ahead of the questing dog through no fault of the dog.

Applicable to Spaniels

Honor: Steady to wing and/or shot of game flushed by a brace mate.

Hup: The command used by trainers to order a spaniel to sit.

Passed Bird: A bird in the area through which a dog has passed and not found.

Punch Out: The action by a flushing dog demonstrating a poor hunting pattern—the dog goes straight out instead of quartering.

Quartering: The necessary back and forth, windshield wiper, hunting pattern which a well-trained spaniel must perform for maximum coverage of a field in bird finding.

Take a Line: The ability and experience to follow the body and foot scent of moving game.

Trailing the Bird Planter: The action of a dog that has learned to follow the scent of the person who improperly planted training birds.

Applicable to Retrievers

Blind Retrieve: Game to be retrieved which the dog could not or did not see fall.

Cold Blind: Game to be retrieved with no shot fired which dog did not see fall. Also, a previously planted, dead bird.

Decoys: Reproductions from plastic, wood or rubber of waterfowl used to attract real birds to shooting areas. Often called *blocks* or *shadows*.

Mark: To observe the exact spot where shot game has fallen.

Marked Fall: Game downed where the dog could observe the fall.

Pop: The voluntary act of a dog, ordered to retrieve, that looks back to its handler for help though not requested to do so. Considered a fault.

Running a Line: The act of following in a straight line the hand signal direction given by the handler when directed to a fall.

Spread: The distance decoys are placed apart or the distance between two or more retrieving bucks placed apart.

Switch Birds: The act of a dog changing one bird for another while retrieving.

Countess Bardlose (1897), an English Setter of Llewellin strain.

Very unsafe, this endangers everyone behind the gunner.

Completely safe, comfortable and ready to take a quick shot if needed.

16

1

Safety Before You Start

THE WILD GAME AND WATERFOWL populations of the U.S. are managed and controlled by the U.S. Fish and Game Service and various state conservation departments. Their joint function is to protect habitat, establish the dates for open hunting seasons and set bag limits. Hunting is a privilege extended to law abiding citizens, but nowhere in the game laws is a hunter permitted to injure a fellow hunter or be shot himself. The basic cause for hunting accidents is gross carelessness in handling a lethal weapon. That behavior is totally inexcusable.

In recent years a number of states have introduced two measures which have contributed to a reduction in hunting accidents. The first is a current program which requires that all first time hunters applying for a license take a 10 hour course in hunting safety and pass an examination before they can receive a license. The second is a requirement that all hunters wear a blaze-orange garment. This eliminates the excuse of novice hunters who say, "I saw something move and thought it was wild game." Both of these measures have produced results as presented on the graph supplied by Gregg Patterson, Editor of the Arkansas Fish and Game monthly magazine. The 1979 high of 15.7% hunting accidents declined 50% to a high of 7.6% in 1985. We believe similar good results have occurred in other states which had introduced blaze-orange outer garments and classroom safety course programs for hunters.

Hunter Education

The Arkansas Hunter Education Program began in 1971. More than 60,000 people have been certified as safe hunters, and according to Game and Fish Commission records only 10 of these graduates have been involved in firearm related hunting accidents.

The Arkansas Game and Fish Commission Hunter Education Course consists of a minimum eight hours classroom instruction in firearm safety, hunter ethics, wildlife conservation and other aspects of the great outdoors. The course is free and open to anyone. The courses are taught throughout the state by volunteer instructors and Game and Fish Commission personnel.

Effective July 1, 1985, it shall be unlawful for anyone born on or after January 1, 1969 to take or attempt to take wildlife with firearms, crossbows, or longbows without first having completed a hunter education course recognized by the Arkansas Game and Fish Commission. Hunters less than 11 years old are excluded from this regulation if they are under the direct supervision of an adult at least 21 years of age.

Every person who is hunting for big game or is in a big game hunting area should wear an outer garment or cap that is brightly colored. *Blaze orange,* also called *hunter orange,* is recommended over the other colors. The bright, fluorescent color can be seen better than other colors, especially at dawn and dusk. Hunter orange cannot be found in nature and does not blend with other colors in nature—that is why it is so effective.

If one has some knowledge of why accidents occur, that knowledge will serve as a partial deterrent to a hunter becoming involved on either side of a hunter/gun accident. We hope that readers will give their full attention to information supplied by Mr. Gregg Patterson of Arkansas Game and Fish magazine.

The types and causes of accidents listed are appalling. At least 90% could be avoided if hunters would learn and practice some safety procedures when they go afield with a lethal weapon. We have asked a sportsman who is a hunter and world-class shotgun wingshot to list some of his personal rules for gun safety. We have hunted with him on many occasions and know from personal experience he is a careful man with a gun. He has never shot anyone in 50 years of hunting, but admits with courage that he was on the receiving end of 22 shotgun pellets 40 years ago when he failed to tell his hunting partner he was going to work out some heavy cover on a Michigan Grouse hunt.

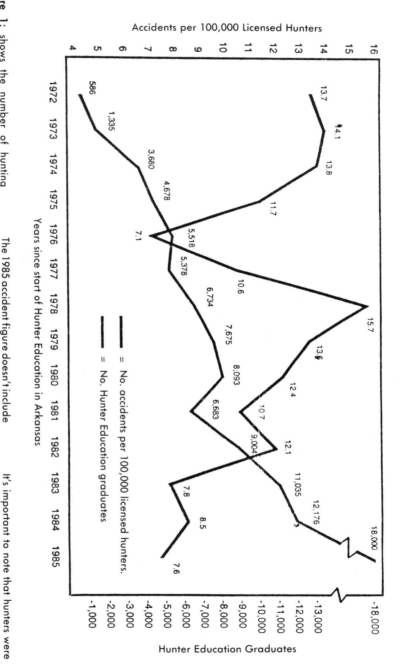

Figure 1: shows the number of hunting accidents and Hunting Education graduates in Arkansas since the program started. Each year runs from July 1st through June 30th.

The 1985 accident figure doesn't include the Spring turkey or squirrel seasons. It's estimated that 18,000 students did complete Hunter Education by June 30, 1985.

It's important to note that hunters were required to wear "Hunter Orange" garments covering at least 400 square inches above the waistline effective May 1, 1975.

Accidents per 100,000 Licensed Hunters

16
15
14
13
12
11
10
9
8
7
6
5
4

Years since start of Hunter Education in Arkansas

1972 1973 1974 1975 1976 1977 1978 1979 1980 1981 1982 1983 1984 1985

13.7
14.1
13.8
11.7
7.1
5,518
5,378
10.6
15.7
13.9
12.4
10.7
12.1
11.035
12.176
7.8
8.5
7.6

586
1,335
3,680
4,678
6,734
7,675
8,093
6,683
9,004
18,000

= No. accidents per 100,000 licensed hunters.

= No. Hunter Education graduates

Hunter Education Graduates

-1,000
-2,000
-3,000
-4,000
-5,000
-6,000
-7,000
-8,000
-9,000
-10,000
-11,000
-12,000
-13,000
-18,000

19

Ernest Wunderlich's credentials include a British record for harvesting 20 consecutive driven Grouse in Scotland and outshooting the field in Spain when pass shooting Blue Pigeons and driven Red-legged Partridge. He has participated as an amateur handler in National Field Trials, served as captain of the guns in perhaps 100 trials and judged many, many such events. A master hunter, he has owned and handled ten field champions. Here are his personal rules for hunting safety:

DO—

1. Learn to carry your gun upside down, on shoulder, as indicated in the photo. If gun is accidentally discharged from this position, it will disperse shot in the air and not in your partner's face.
2. Carry gun in case and unloaded when traveling in an automobile.
3. Inspect gun barrel before loading to remove any blockage.
4. Appoint one person as gun captain. This will enable someone to establish procedures and enforce them verbally if they are violated.
5. Maintain visual or vocal contact when hunting in high cover.
6. When hunting in tall cover with blockers at the end of the field, establish signals so that hunters can alert each other when in gun range.
7. Separate hunters 75 or more yards apart when pass or jump shooting.
8. Exercise caution when shooting birds at a public or private club. Pass up weak birds under 10 feet in the air.
9. Unload gun when entering car or any enclosure or moving to a new area.
10. Treat every gun as if it were loaded, even if you think it is not.
11. Obey all game laws, so your grandchildren can enjoy hunting too.

DON'T—

1. Leave dog in car even with the windows cracked. The sun can increase the temperature to over 100 degrees in less than 15 minutes.
2. Fire gun more than 10 degrees to either side when in a hunting party. A shot may dart 15 or more degrees to the side, striking another member of the party.

20

3. Carry different gauge shells. Loading the wrong size shell has caused many serious injuries.
4. Cross fences with loaded guns. Partners should hold weapons while one person crosses.
5. Lean a loaded weapon against anything. Knocking it over can cause it to discharge.
6. Remove a gun from an enclosure by grasping the barrel. Always lift gun by stock with barrel elevated.

The Gordon Setter, MacGeowl's Braird, winner of a Gordon shooting stake, is a typical representative of this breed. The Gordon makes an exceptional personal shooting dog where speed is not a critical factor.

Veteran Brittany fancier John Doak and his fine field dog Barney Bazooka. Doak raises his hat during a field trial to signal the judges that Barney has found and is pointing birds.

John Olin shoulders his Winchester model 21 to fire at a single quail that lifted before a staunch point and back by two good Pointers. The scene is Nilo Plantation in Georgia.

2

What All Gun Dogs
Should Know

THE OBJECTIVES OF THIS BOOK are to provide specific knowledge of, and field training techniques for, three generic breed types of gun dogs: pointing dogs, spaniels and retrievers. This manual is oriented in the direction of hunters who want to own and train a hunting dog for the first time, for experienced hunters who want to brush up on training techniques, and for hunters who want to know if they have the right dogs for their favorite game bird hunting.

Educating a gun dog of any breed to perform well in the field is both an art and a skill, and a most rewarding hobby enjoyed by many of the twenty million holders of hunting licenses for six or eight months each year. The rewards and pleasure come from two directions. The first is the personal satisfaction of developing a live, eager puppy into a polished, two-year-old hunting partner who loves his work as much as his hunter owner. The second is the personal satisfaction the owner receives from the contribution a trained dog can make to game conservation. A trained gun dog of any breed conserves game by finding all the game shot, thus reducing the quantity of game the hunter shoots to fill his limit. And this means more native game and breeding stock left as seed for preservation of the several species.

The following contents and organization describe how each breed type performs before the gun and offers some suggestions for selecting a puppy with the instincts and temperament to become a satisfactory gun dog. This book details practical methods for training the newly arrived youngster from puppy to adult. It also tells how owner/trainers and their dogs in any of the several breeds can gain much practical experience and have a bushel of fun in the highly exciting sport of field trials.

IMPORTANT! For each breed type—pointing dogs, spaniels and retrievers—the instructions are preceded by an outline for the sequence of training. This outline gives the reader a quick bird's eye view of the steps he will take in training his dog from eight weeks of age to maturity. Each outline is then followed by fully detailed and specific instructions for every training routine.

One group of animal behaviorists who have attempted to measure the relative intelligence of the numerous species, which Marlin Perkins calls the "Wild Kingdom," lists the Primates (the great apes) as the most intelligent. In second place are the Carnivores (dogs, cats, etc.). Just behind them in third place are the Ungulates (horses, elephants, etc.). Following in descending order are birds, reptiles, amphibians and fish. Dog owners can therefore be assured that some scientists confirm the opinion, well known by every dog trainer, that Spot has the intelligence to learn and remember the several training routines he must master to become a satisfactory gun dog. The scientists also know that certain actions and experiences to which dogs may be exposed can exert a strong influence on behavior. They refer to such experiences as reinforcers which may encourage either desirable or improper behavior. Since science and logic are in total agreement here, it follows that the wise trainer will be over-generous in rewarding (much petting and verbal praise) the young dog when he responds correctly to each act in any training routine, because petting and praise are great reinforcers. By the same logic the trainer will inflict only mild and gentle punishment (harsh words or a shake or two of the collar) to the young dog and then only when he knows positively that young Spot knows and understands what is expected of him. Reinforcers for desirable behavior should be used throughout the dog's life in all circumstances, but may be gradually reduced from over-generous praise for the youngster to a verbal "good boy" and one or two pats on the head as the dog becomes older.

It may appear that there is some repetition in the chapters describing the training routines for the three breed types. Perhaps there is, but since the suggested routines are somewhat different in technique and do not follow the same exact sequence for the three types, the repetition is considered necessary. For example, a pointing dog should develop an independence in his search for game and learn to hunt the birdy places, often on the edge of cover or objectives. The spaniel should learn to hunt by quartering back and forth on a 60 to 70 yard front and be a beater rather than an independent hunter. Retrievers should become good line runners and move out fast on a straight line when given a direction. Obviously, one can't train each of the three types with the same technique or in the same exact sequence of routines.

First and foremost, every gun dog must possess a strong desire and love to hunt and find game because, regardless of good training, without hunting desire he is useless. Of equal importance, he must be obedient. If his natural ability and desire cannot be controlled, or he hunts for himself rather than to the gun, he is also useless. And his obedience must be based on respect and NOT fear. The fearful dog is not only an unattractive worker but often demonstrates highly undesirable characteristics, such as blinking game (avoiding it), bolting (departing from training or hunting sessions to hunt for himself or return to the kennel), or even hard mouth (crushing or eating shot game he is expected to retrieve). And finally, the complete hunting dog must possess the ability to retrieve all shot game in a satisfactory manner. Failure to retrieve properly reduces the hunter's satisfaction in completing the three basic actions in the hunting cycle of locating, shooting and collecting all game shot. More important, the hunter who leaves more than three or four percent of shot or crippled game in the field has the same inexcusable effect on ecology and game population as the meat hog who persistently takes more than the legal limit. To the three basics of good hunting desire, obedience and ability to retrieve must be added the sagacity to know where to hunt and to search for shot game. Obviously, the complete finished hunting dog must know a good many other things, many of which he will acquire from learning the four basics and with experience in the field.

Methods of teaching certain responses through proven training routines are outlined in the book along with suggested sequence age brackets for the several breeds. But if the text seems to indicate that an unreasonable amount of time is required to convert or mold a puppy into a trained 18-months-old gun dog, the necessary time requirement will fall into perspective if one understands that it can be done in less than 120 hours (not consecutive hours). And what dedicated golfer, skeet shooter or avid fisherman spends less than the equivalent of three 40-hour work weeks becoming proficient at his sport in a span of 18 months' time?

Double (1985-1986) NGSPA National Champion Luckenwilde's Thunder owned by Fred Krenc of Ohio and handled by Steger of Illinois, stands tall and proud in bird cover. Thunder has won three additional All-Age Regional Championships, an imposing win record. *National German Shorthaired Pointer Association*

3

Choosing the Correct Gun Dog—The Breeds and Breeding

ALL DOGS WILL HUNT and so will their blood cousins the wolves, but a modern hunter would never acquire a wolf to hunt upland game or retrieve waterfowl even though the wolf has sustained life by hunting for a thousand years and more. The question which concerns the hunter is not will he hunt, but how he hunts. The gun dog breeds have skills and aptitudes built into their genetic structure by hundreds of years of selective breeding. Just as important as breeding is the testing of offspring to learn if these special aptitudes and skills were handed down in enough intensity to make them good gun dogs.

One pitfall the novice hunter must avoid is a prospect with the correct breed name but the incorrect breeding. It has long been established that the Pointer, the English Setter, the English Springer Spaniel, the Labrador Retriever and almost every popular gun dog breed converted to bench show dogs is bred and judged solely on physical conformation. This means that most show dogs have not been tested in the field for several generations on their aptitude and ability to perform as creditable gun dogs. One sure way to identify a field-bred gun dog is to check a five generation pedigree which indicates the number and quality of field trial placements of the

Ch. Volcanic Express locked up high and tight on quail at Aimes Plantation enroute to winning the 1975 National Open Championship for Pointing Dogs. He is owned by Dr. and Mrs. W. L. Humphries and handled by Marion Gordon. *Harry Reynolds, Memphis Commercial Appeal*

ancestors. A reputable breeder will always advise if his dogs are field-bred. Show dogs may have had field-bred ancestors far back in their pedigrees, but if said ancestors have been kept out of the field and not tested in each generation, they are a poor risk as gun dog prospects. The testing is important because desirable genes may skip a generation. Therefore each generation and each individual dog used for breeding must actually be tested in the field if his offspring are offered as good gun dog prospects.

To fully describe the difference in hunting behavior and style of pointing dogs and flushing dogs, we will discuss how they should work in three different types of cover found in many sections of the United States.

The sporting dogs of the United States, used primarily on upland game and waterfowl and discussed in this book, fall into three classifications based on their manner of hunting and handling game. They are the pointing, the flushing and the retrieving breeds. The largest group are the pointing breeds, listed below in the order of their popularity with field trailers in the combined, official stud book records of the American Field Publishing Company of Chicago and the American Kennel Club of New York:

The Pointing Breeds

> The Pointer
> The Brittany
> The German Shorthaired Pointer
> The English Setter
> The Irish Setter
> The Weimaraner
> The Vizsla
> The Gordon Setter

Two other pointing breeds for which it was difficult to obtain statistical data are the German Wirehaired Pointer and the Wirehaired Pointing Griffon. To put the above popularity ratings in perspective, one should know that the Pointers outdistanced the second and third place Brittanys and German Shorthaired Pointers by more than 40% and the tail-end Gordon Setters by 1000%.

The Retriever Breeds

> The Labrador Retriever
> The Golden Retriever
> The Chesapeake Bay Retriever

Other retriever breeds, seldom seen in a duck blind or field trial, are the Curly- and Flat-Coated Retrievers, the Irish Water Spaniel, and the American Water Spaniel.

The Flushing Land Spaniels

The English Springer Spaniel
The Welsh Springer Spaniel
The Cocker Spaniel—English and American

The aggressive but tractable Springer Spaniel has virtually replaced the other flushing spaniels as hunting and field trial dogs. A generation ago one saw both American and English Cockers—and to a lesser extent Clumbers, Field and Sussex Spaniels—in trials and the hunting fields. Modern day British, Canadian and American breeders, who concentrated their efforts on producing a superb total gun dog, have by their efforts relegated the other spaniel breeds to the not necessarily undesirable position of show dogs and family pets. They are seldom seen in the field and never in the United States spaniel field trials. However, the routines outlined for training Springers can be used for training any spaniel or flushing dog.

What Are Field Trials?

Field Trials for the several breeds are competitive tests of a gun dog's hunting and sometimes retrieving skills on native or released game birds in competition with others of the same breed type under the judgment of two or three experienced judges. In general, the performance should resemble that of an ordinary day's shooting except that in trials a dog should do his work in a more nearly perfect manner, exhibiting superior game finding ability and precision control.

Field trials for the several breeds make two major contributions to the sporting dog public. They provide many hours of most pleasant, fruitful and challenging recreation to thousands of hunters in a healthy outdoor sport. They also improve the native ability of the several breeds to a measurable degree, as does competition in other competitive sports. And, in each breed there is much beneficial fall out for the hunting man from the great reservoir of proven blood lines, from trial winners, to insure that the next puppy he buys or stud to which he breeds has the desirable characteristics for producing superior gun dogs. Another specific benefit contributes

30

The Brittany, National and Dual Ch. Pacolet Cheyenne Sam, owned by Ken Jacobson, on a soul-stirring point. Sam is a Canadian field champion and the winner of an international endurance championship for pointing dogs. He has also sired a host of good personal shooting dogs, trial and bench winners. He mirrors the breed ideal of a dog who can work in the field and win in the showring.

1985 National NGSPA Shooting Dog Champion Leipchen Buddendorf owned by Mary Finley, handler Ed Husser. Leipchen has Double (1985-1986) National Shorthaired All-Age Championships plus several regional championship titles. *Mike Aldrich*
Sect. N.G.SH.P Association

1986 National Amateur Pheasant Shooting Dog Champion—Oliver's Warhoop Jane, owned by Stephen C. Walker and K. B. Menish of California. Jane, handled by Stephen Walker, has won five championships and five runner-up placements.

1986 Champion Scarlet Feaver locked up in a stylish point. She is an Irish Setter commonly known as Red Setter. Feaver is owned by Roger W. Boser, D.V.M.

The English Setter, National Ch. Johnny Crockett; owned by H. P. Sheely and handled to the title by W. C. Kirk, was the first of his breed to win the National Open title since 1946. Prior to Johnny's untimely death, a quantity of his semen was frozen by Dr. S. W. J. Seager, then a faculty member of the University of Oregon Medical School. A number of live litters have since resulted, hopefully perpetuating this dog's fine heritage.

to the welfare of the general public and hunters in the conservation and propagation of wild life and ecology through the money and effort expended by hunters and field trialers in preserving habitat for wildlife, State Parks and open expanses of country. Field trialing is a great sport for the amateur trainer-owner-handler. In 1975 the National Open Championships for both retrievers and Springer Spaniels were won by amateurs who licked the nation's top professionals in each sport.

The Pointing Breeds

The three most prevalent types of cover and the manner in which a pointing dog works them are:

1. Agriculture grain areas where small grain crops are the main and widely grown product. Consists of portions of the central United States from the Canadian border to sections of the southern states, like Texas, Louisiana, and the Carolinas.
2. Large areas of open country where grazing and livestock raising is the principal product and use of the land. Land adjacent to the great plains and extending to sections of those plains in Kansas, Nebraska, eastern Colorado, Texas, and Oklahoma.
3. Rolling country which in some areas could range from slight hills to foothills of mountains. Pennsylvania, the Ozarks, Virginia, and sections of many western states as well as portions of New England, southern Illinois, Indiana, Ohio, and on to the Pacific ocean could be included.

In agriculture grain areas, pointing dogs learn to follow upland game birds. Those found in largest numbers are Bobwhite Quail, and Pheasant. The Quail are edge birds spending much of their time feeding, resting, dusting or sunning on edges of grain stubble fields, weed fields, timber, fences, or ditches. They leave the roost soon after daylight heading for feeding areas, then move to an edge adjacent to cover for rest. In mid-afternoon they feed again, then go to roost.

The Pheasant has a similar routine. He feeds in standing grain or beans, then rests in cover. He will feed again in the afternoon and return to roost at night. During hunting season he may hole up in a slough edge or heavy sweet clover field.

The pointing dog learns to work grain field terrain by going from birdy edge objectives to another birdy objective of timber, heavy fence row or standing grain. With experience, his memory improves and he becomes self-trained to search the objectives with handler's help.

In grazing or stock raising country, the pointing dogs probably widen their search area and make long sweeping casts from side to side, heading toward the occasional objective of a fence row, timber line, ditch, or creek bank. Such country is made for dogs who like to run.

In the rough rolling country, the experienced pointing dog will probably shorten his range a bit and his sweeping casts as well. If there are birdy objectives he will check them out, but his pattern will usually not be as fixed as in other terrains.

The leading pointing dog breeds favored by hunters on this continent are the end result of highly selective breeding. Practical breeders accelerate the genetic theory of "survival of the fittest" by breeding the best to the best and destroying those which demonstrated less intensity of the desirable traits.

This is especially true of the first four pointing breeds listed. The Pointer and the English Setter from field-bred stock have been bred for more than one hundred years to produce both the wide ranging dogs of great endurance for the larger hunting areas of the South and West and the closer working dogs for the smaller hunting country of the North and East. Thus the buyer of either breed can find a dog adaptable to the geography of the hunting country in his area.

The German Shorthaired Pointer and the Brittany have experienced phenomenal growth in popularity since their mass introduction to North America following World War II. They were bred as close workers for the smaller hunting fields of the British Isles and the European continent and many of them still possess this characteristic. However, American hunters and field trialers developed strains of Brittanys and Shorthairs which are approaching the range of the Pointer and English Setter.

The Weimaraner, another import from Germany and slightly oversold by returning GIs, has made some inroads on the popularity of other breeds whose hunting pattern is considered close to medium range.

The Irish Setter with his lovely mahogany coat suffered a

decline in the first half of this century when he was adopted in great numbers because of his physical beauty by the showdog fancy. In recent years serious breeders have made considerable strides in bringing him back to his former glory as a fine gun dog.

The Vizsla, a recent import from Hungary, is showing promise as a good, close-working gun dog, as is the German Wirehaired Pointer formerly known as a Draathaar. Both are presently more popular with hunters than the handsome, black and tan Gordon Setter, which has lost much of his early 20th century favor with hunters.

There are breeds and a bloodline of pointing dogs to fill the need of every hunter whether he is mounted on a Tennessee walking horse in the big plantation country of the South or walking behind his dog in close, brushy country or a shooting preserve of other sections. Typically, pointing dogs hunt with a high head and on scenting game, freeze instantly in a rigid, solid point indicating the game's location by the position of their bodies. They are trained to hold point until the hunter walks ahead and flushes the game. Most hunting dogs will give chase when the game is flushed and are expected to retrieve dead and crippled birds. Dogs competing in most field trial stakes are not asked to retrieve but are expected to be steady to shot and flush. After the point is first established and the game then moves, the well trained dog will remain frozen on point until ordered to relocate, whereupon he will move on, find and point the game again. If the handler and a friend are working two or more dogs at the same time and one dog establishes a point, the others are expected to honor the first dog by backing (pointing the game finder). This oversimplified description of working bird dogs describes only the basic action. It says nothing about the thrill of casting a pair of fine dogs into game-holding cover and seeing them race off to birdy objectives which experience has taught them should contain game. As they split with one racing on the downwind side of a fence row and the other moving speedily down a timber, grain field or stubble edge with head high and tail cracking, the sight is sure to release a little adrenalin into even the most phlegmatic hunter's blood. The action quickens as one of the pair suddenly swings upwind and, after a short, intense run, explodes into a solid, lofty point. When the bracemate, still whizzing along sees the other dog on point and instantly skids to a spine-tingling honor of the first dog's find, even a blind man might sense the thrill and romance of

The Irish Setter, Saturday Night Zeke, owned by Professor Reuel Pietz, runner up at the 1972 National Red Setter Championship and winner in 1974, typifies the modern field-bred Irish Setter.

A young Weimaraner on point in the typical style of the breed. This member of the continental pointer family first appeared in the United States in 1929. He is highly intelligent, very amenable to training and makes an excellent personal shooting dog.

The German Wirehaired Pointer, Heywire's Windstorm, bred by Judy Cheshire and owned by Donna Kraft, Beverly Murray and Judy Cheshire. "Clint," his owner's personal shooting dog, promises to be one of those rare dual dogs, for even as a puppy he has scored successes both in the field and the breed ring.

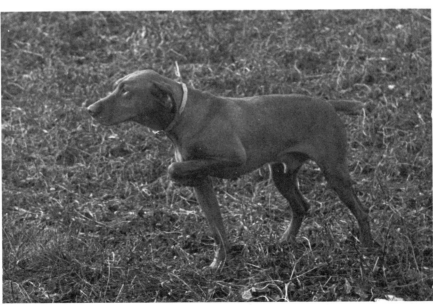

The Vizsla, Ch. Hubertus Aprod. This Hungarian breed is a fine, close-working continental pointer.

shooting over fine gun dogs. The satisfaction for the owner is compounded if he trained one or both of the dogs to perform in this manner—especially if two birds in the covey rise are shot and both are retrieved with unruffled feathers by the dogs.

How Spaniels Hunt to the Gun

It is a moot question which came first, the spaniels or the pointing dogs. The early ancestors of both are thought by ancient authorities to have originated in Spain or at least somewhere on the continent of Europe. But it took long years of selective breeding by early and more recent hunters to bring both breed types to their present degree of near perfection. One obstacle the shooting man had to overcome is the influence of the show breeders who, in the middle of the last century, set up arbitrary physical standards of how they thought a good hunting dog should be put together. Practical-minded hunters who were more interested in performance than in physical appearance have solved this problem in some breeds by breeding only proven hunting dogs to other proven hunting dogs. The show fanciers followed the same procedure and bred dogs which fit their manmade standards. As a consequence in some breeds the two types are so far apart that they are almost two distinct breeds even though classified under the same breed name. The English Springer Spaniel is a perfect example of this schism with smaller, quicker, more alert field-bred strains as far ahead of their larger, slower, more massive show-bred cousins in hunting as a Tennessee Walking horse is superior to a Clydesdale horse for saddle purposes.

The English Springer Spaniel of field-bred bloodlines is virtually the last of the formerly large family of flushing gun dogs so popular with hunters fifty years ago. His closest rival as a flushing dog which works before the gun is probably one of the retriever breeds. But the quick, eager, 35-pound Springer will cover more ground faster and hit briar infested, brushy cover more eagerly than the larger 70-pound retriever. The Springer can penetrate a multi-floral, hog-tight rose hedge that a big Labrador can hardly get a foot through. And the Springer will find and fetch birds shot by foot hunters just as well as a retriever.

The Springer, which finds and flushes or springs game into flight rather than pointing it, is the modern product of the several breeds of ancient land spaniels. He is the leading contender for the title of all 'round gun dog. He is bred and trained to work within gun range and to find and flush both feathers and fur. He is considered by competent authority as the world's best pheasant dog and is a remarkable retriever from both land and water. The trained Springer will quarter the ground to each side of the hunter (crossing slightly to the front) to a maximum distance of 30 to 40 yards. His working pattern on land can be described as a sweeping action similar to the motion of an automobile's windshield wiper. He is a beater who works with high head searching for both body and foot scent. When game is contacted (either bird or rabbit) he will dive in quickly with great animation—tail buzzing and ears flopping—and force game to fly or flee. A completely trained spaniel will then hup (sit) at the instant of flush and retrieve dead or crippled game only on command. When his nose tells him that he has struck the line (scent) of moving game he will follow the line at considerable speed until game is found and flushed, or until the handler stops him at the edge of gun range. When this occurs, the handler will walk up to the dog, order him back on line and repeat this action until game is eventually cornered and flushed.

The Springer is a good waterfowl dog for use in duck blind or in jump shooting in a marsh. When in the blind, he will sit quietly until one or more ducks or geese have been downed, and retrieve them on command. He quickly learns to take hand-signal directions for game he did not mark.

The Flushing Breeds

The Springers and the retrievers, when used to hunt before the gun on upland game, must be trained to quarter back and forth in front of hunters on a 50-60 yard front, always within shotgun range. If several hunters are driving a field several yards apart, an experienced flushing dog will soon learn to increase his range and work ten or more yards outside each of the people on the outside of the advancing group. One can say that regardless of the cover or terrain, the flushing dog is a beater and not a free hunter like a pointing dog. Obviously a flusher must hunt within gun range, since the birds he flushes 70 or 80 yards ahead or to the side of the nearest gun are lost. It requires a super wing shot and an extra tightly bored twelve gauge shotgun to kill a game bird at more than 60 yards. Also, not a little but a lot of luck and a golden pellet are necessary to bring down game at greater distance than 60 yards.

Flushing dogs which are trained to work as non-slip retrieving dogs become great line runners in hunting or Retriever Field Trials.

Double National Open Champion Wind Riding Streak (1982 & 1984) owned by Drs. Mark and Aileen Schinderle of Michigan. Streak also earned Field Champion and Amateur Field Champion titles enroute to his two National Open Championships. He was handled to all titles by Dr. Mark Schinderle.

1985 National Amateur Field Champion Marchfield's Tucker posed with trophies and proud owner Leslie Girling, Winnipeg, Canada. Les Girling cannot only train at the National Championship level, he can breed dogs at that level. Tucker's sire, a Canadian National Field Champion, had both U.S. Open and Amateur Championships to his credit and was handled by Girling to all three titles.

1985 Retriever National Champion Dynamite Duke 4th, owned by Dr. Marshall & Linden Dunaway, handled by Hugh Arthur. This great Labrador out-performed a field of 66 to win the National title. Dr. Dunaway handled Duke to an Amateur Championship prior to his win of the National title.

The late Martin J. Hogan, Dean of the professional trainers on two continents during the first half of this century. With him are five of his pupils. They are (from left) a Labrador Retriever, a Clumber Spaniel, a Cocker Spaniel, an Airedale Terrier and a Golden Retriever.

Line running for a flushing dog means the dog takes a straight line for a bird he has seen fall, for a blind retrieve (dog did not see the bird fall), or a cold blind retrieve (dog did not see the bird fall or hear a shot), being directed only by voice and hand signals.

The retriever breeds are also specialists at line running retrieving. A retriever field trial is a good place to see dogs perform this activity in a super manner. Cold blind falls occasionally in excess of 200 yards are not uncommon. As a long time amateur gun dog trainer and hunter of upland game and waterfowl for more than fifty years, I never cease to be impressed at the blind retrieves made in field trials.

It is interesting to note that some retriever field trial people are taking a new interest in teaching retrievers to quarter before the gun. Two articles have appeared in the publication *The Retriever Field Trial News* (May 1986) entitled "Taking a line or Quartering," by Vel Walker. We believe Mr. Walker is aware that hunters who use retrievers on upland game have wanted their dogs to quarter. For many years Springers have been doing it in England, America and other countries since the invention of the percussion cap for muzzle loaders, which made wing shooting possible.

How Retrievers Hunt

The several retriever breeds are exactly what the name implies— magnificent retrieving specialists, the origin of which has been credited to many countries. The ancient foundation stock for some of them is credited to the extremely ancient Water Spaniel of Great Britain. Modern day hunters have made the Labrador Retriever the undisputed leader of the several retriever breeds. His origin is hidden. Some authorities credit it to Newfoundland fishermen, but there is little doubt that the Labrador came to full flower as a superior gun dog in England, and was brought to North America in increasing numbers in the second and third decades of this century to become the number one retriever breed in the American Kennel Club registrations for the past 20 years.

The Irish Water Spaniel developed in Ireland in the last century, and the Chesapeake Bay Retriever which some authorities attribute to American origin, were the favorite duck dogs of the market hunter of the last century and the first quarter of the 20th century. Long and/or short shooting seasons and bag limits attracted market hunters as well as hunters to the waterfowl marshes of the four U.S. flyways. Good hunters, as always, wanted to save the cripples, but the market hunter was motivated by the cash he received for the game he shot. Both parties placed great dependence on the Irishman and the Chesapeake Bay dogs to retrieve day after day in the cold waters of the ocean and the inland rivers and lakes. But along with the Labrador, the Golden Retriever, of Scottish origin, soon replaced the Irish and Chesapeake dogs with U.S. waterfowl hunters. Much of the quick rise in popularity of these two breeds is attributed to their exposure and the success they achieved in the first field trials for retrievers in the United States during the early 1930's.

Labradors have dominated the trials with their drive, speed and tractability, with Goldens in a not very close second, and wise hunters soon got the word. Presently their kind are seen in thousands of duck marshes and flyway shoots in every state in the Union.

The smallest of the retrievers is the American Water Spaniel. He has almost disappeared from the scene, and the Curly-Coated and Flat-Coated Retrievers never really got off the ground as duck dogs or field trial winners in America.

The number one function of any retriever is to find and fetch upland game or waterfowl shot by the hunter. He should sit or lie quietly in a blind or boat and remain there without movement or noise until ordered to retrieve one or more downed birds with a soft carry. Hard-mouthed gun dogs of any breed, which crush or mash game, are not desirable. Most retrievers have a soft mouth resulting from years of careful breeding. Retrievers have the native ability to become excellent markers of falling game and can spot movement at great distance. They also have considerable ability to remember the location of one or more downed birds. If permitted to watch the action through a small peephole in the blind, they will learn to mark and, with experience, remember the fall for considerable periods of time. Selective breeding, especially in Labradors and Goldens, has imprinted on these breeds not only a friendly disposition but the ability to accept training and to handle kindly. In these days of small bag limits and reduced waterfowl populations, this is a plus benefit to the hunter who often waits to collect one or more dead birds until a lull occurs in the morning or evening flight. A dog which will take hand-signal directions to a distant spot where a dead bird has drifted or a cripple has taken cover is a most valuable aid to the gun. Not only does his owner derive much satisfaction from having his dog fetch a cripple, which may have moved 150 yards from the original fall, but he contributes to good game conservation by collecting ALL the game which has fallen to his gun. Good retrieving dogs are game conservationists. And with the proposal to replace lead with iron shot in the offing, which some researchers believe will bring an increase in cripples, a good retriever is bound to score even more points with conservationists.

Hunting upland game, with the retriever at heel or hunting out in front like a spaniel, is a most important function of the several retriever breeds. When used primarily as a non-slip dog at heel, he should mark all fallen game accurately and fetch it only on command. With experience, he will learn to do it quickly. It is virtually impossible to lose a four-pound, crippled cock pheasant, which legs it down a corn row, because the good hunting retriever will follow the line of scent and eventually come up with even the strongest wing-tipped runner if scenting is normal. When asked to work as a flushing dog before the gun his performance will be satisfactory in finding and flushing though it will not have the dash and snap of a spaniel's. He can plow through the muck of a cat-tail swamp with power and strength to push out waterfowl or gamey shore birds for sporty jump shooting, or ride, quietly alert, in a duck boat. He can handle fast water in a river or cold water in any climate better than a spaniel. And he will fill the game bag with either fur or feather by fast, accurate retrieves of any game the hunter can get down, dead or crippled.

The gallery at cast-off time during an Illinois Shooting Dog championship field trial. In a trial for pointing dogs, access to a horse is essential because of the speed and range of the dogs. Spectators who do not own horses rent them for the occasion. Club officials, judges and handlers must also be on horseback to keep up with the action. *Illinois Department of Conservation*

These German Wirehaired Pointer puppies show a keen interest in visitors as they stand up to look out from their pen. This eagerness will help to make them good gun dog prospects.

Two eight-week-old Pointer puppies, owned by Don Frizell, sight pointing a piece of cloth which is being dangled between them on the end of a fishing rod. *Goodall*

4

How to Select a Gun Dog Puppy

THE SELECTION OF A GUN DOG PUPPY slightly resembles forecasting the weather. The experts always have an opinion, but they are not always right. They are correct often enough to make it worthwhile to have some degree of confidence in their forecasts. And there are certain bits of evidence available which one can observe even in a six-weeks-old youngster to indicate desirable and undesirable traits.

The first decision the prospective owner-trainer must make is which one of the three sporting types—pointing dogs, spaniels, or retrievers—is best suited for said owner's favorite hunting. Then he must decide which individual breed in the retriever, spaniel, or pointing dog families will do the best job on the game which predominates in his hunting areas. But since before making that decision the prospective owner may wish to delve deeper into the typical, specialized hunting characteristics of the three generic breeds—pointers, spaniels or retrievers—a discussion of what good points to look for, and what bad ones to avoid, in any gun dog prospect is in order.

The first important fact to be determined by the buyer is: Were the parents of this puppy from field bred, hunting stock whose ancestors were hunting or field trial dogs for several generations? It's true that all dogs will hunt to a degree, but so will house cats and foxes. How they hunt is highly important. Wise breeders gave a helping hand to nature and to the genetic principle of survival of the fittest by careful selection and serious testing of dogs in the field before using them as breeding stock. A puppy from a litter whose close-up ancestors had some field trial wins or were top hunting dogs gives some assurance that he probably has acceptable breeding.

William F. Brown—a long time, dedicated, recognized gun dog authority and Editor of *The American Field* which was established in 1874—has this to say about the importance of breeding: "History discloses that the great gun dogs of any breed come from dynamic, aggressive, prepotent individuals. Without these brilliant, scintillating, spectacular, hard driving, independent performers, consumed with a passion for finding birds, evincing unquestionable fire in the quest, needing restraint rather than encouragement but possessing the temperament to accept training, the splendid shooting dogs of the current era could not have been bred and developed."

The first physical and mental trait to look for in a puppy is boldness in the kennel and yard. Does he rush out of his house and jump upon the wire and show keen interest in visitors, his kennel mates and all the action that occurs? If a finger is poked through the wire he should lick it or chew it and enjoy the contact. A puppy may even seize a rock or stick and carry it proudly around the kennel or yard and join in a puppy game of "keep away" with one or more kennel mates. If released from the kennel run he will probably chase after a thrown handkerchief or other object and bring it back to the thrower or dart off to one side and bury it in some leaves. A pointing dog puppy might sight-point a bird, or bug or butterfly, and be bold and happy and in the center of the kennel action most of the time. If released from the kennel and tempted with a bird wing or shiny object dangled from a casting rod, he might freeze momentarily in a tense sight-point. This is often an indication of his desire or future style (high or low head—high or low tail) on game. Like the weatherman's forecasts, these simple behavior characteristics are not positive guarantees of his future behavior, but they are indications.

The shy one, who peeks out of his kennel house or slinks around the kennel yard with tucked-in tail, or cringes at a loud noise or spooks if someone moves a hand or foot, is a poor risk. And so is the biter or serious growler (at eight or ten weeks of age), or the placid one who is not interested in humans or his kennel mates and ignores the birds and the bees.

The color of an individual puppy is not a good measure of the dog's prospective ability as a gun dog, except in the negative sense that it may indicate the litter is not pure-bred. Certainly a solid red Springer Spaniel or a white Labrador Retriever would be a red flag to any buyer. If one has doubts or lack of knowledge about the typical and predominant colors of any breed a little research in breed publications, such as *The American Field, The Flushing Whip, The Springer Bark, The American Brittany Hunting Dog* or other good breed publications whose addresses will be found in the Bibliography will be most helpful. Certain breed books also listed can provide much worthwhile knowledge about the individual breeds.

The mental traits or intelligence of a puppy are more difficult to determine. The prospective owner can usually acquire some evidence by inquiring about the ancestors. If they were good hunting dogs or the five generation pedigree is sprinkled with field trial Field Champion prefixes or field trial winners, he at least knows the family had enough intelligence to accept and retain a great deal of training.

The owner of the litter can often be expected to describe the parents as either wide or close hunters if they are pointing dogs, and may, upon request, arrange for a short demonstration in the field of one or both parents. Some serious reading of breed publications and much conversation with veteran, amateur or professional trainers are highly recommended to any prospective owner, whether novice or veteran.

The 1986 National Champion pointing dog Bluff City Mike, owned by Robert E. (Bob) Wallace of Tennessee, was handled to this prestigious title by professional Tommy Davis. His win record includes three other Championship trials and several more All-Age Open stakes. This trial has been recognized as the top event for bird dogs in the U.S. since the first National was held in 1896.   *Henry Reynolds*
                                                                                                                    Memphis Commercial Appeal

1986 National Open Shooting Dog Champion Carden Bottom Lady, owned by John Cole and handled by Gordon Hazelwood. Cole's first dog, she won a National Championship which hundreds of gun dog enthusiasts have not done in 20 years of competition.

5

How to Train Pointing Dogs

THERE ARE ONLY THREE broad basic character-istics a good pointing dog must possess:

> How and where to hunt and find game with desire, sagacity and controlled objective searching. The discipline to respond to all commands at all times. The ability and desire to find and to retrieve shot game with polish and good manners.

These, reduced to their lowest common denominator, are the attributes of a finished, polished hunting dog of a pointing breed. Any hunter willing to devote 120 hours, interspersed over a period of 12 to 18 months, can achieve these gratifying goals by converting a puppy into a satisfactory hunting dog. But in the process dog and trainer will greatly expand their knowledge and comprehension of hunting and of canine behavior beyond any superficial meaning conveyed in the above, oversimplified descriptions. For example, when a child learns to walk and talk he has learned much more than just the ability to become mobile and to communicate. And so will the puppy. He, too, will expand his knowledge and ability to cope with many situations from the experience gained from learning the several suggested training routines presented herein.

Here, for a quick bird's eye view, is the suggested age training sequence for pointing dogs:

Eight to Twelve Weeks of Age—Early Yard Work

1. Teach puppy his name and socialize him with several daily play periods.
2. Introduce flipped bird wing to arouse pointing instinct.
3. Early lessons in COME and WHOA responses but no pressure.
4. Begin early retrieving with knotted hand towel, then switch to small canvas buck (boat bumper). Use cap pistol and/or hand clap when object is thrown.

Three to Six Months of Age

1. Continue above routines daily or at least three times weekly.
2. Switch to large canvas boat bumper and hard buck in retrieving routine.
3. Teach dog COME, KENNEL UP, NO and to remain in the car or crate until given command to unload. Begin with voice signals and work in whistle and hand signals.
4. Begin trips to the field and encourage puppy to find, flash point, flush and chase. Fire cap pistol. Style up before releasing to hunt and send with two short blasts of the whistle.
5. Teach puppy to WHOA—first with verbal command, then with raised arm signal.
6. Begin routine to steady puppy to thrown retrieving buck—yard only.
7. Work dog in field containing game at least once a week—early or late best time of day.

Six to Nine Months of Age

1. Continue yard work at least twice weekly. Require perfect response to all voice, whistle and hand commands and signals.
2. Include dead, cold pigeons in retrieving with pistol shot each time.
3. Work dog on native game in the field at every opportunity.
4. Shoot live pigeons with dog whoaed at heel, which he retrieves only on command. Use checkcord as insurance.

Ten to Twelve Months of Age

1. Continue yard work at least once a week.
2. When signs are right begin to staunch dog while on point (no more flushing and chasing). Begin with pigeons and switch to released or planted game birds when O.K. on pigeons. Concentrate on this until the dog is staunch on planted birds.

Thirteen to Eighteen Months of Age

1. Continue yard work at least once a week.
2. If dog has been 100% staunch for two months on released game birds, test on wild, native birds with which he should be staunch 95% of the time.
3. Steady dog to flush and shot when staunch all the time. Begin by shooting more live pigeons with dog at heel and retrieving only on command.
4. Work dog with checkcord attached on planted or rolled-in pigeons, or birds on pigeon pole. Force him to remain at WHOA and styled up on point after the bird is flushed. No retrieving on first 24 birds, so pistol can be used.
5. Switch from pigeons to planted game birds (quail, pheasant, chukars) when steady on pigeons for several weeks. Dog not asked to retrieve at this point, but pistol should be fired when game is flushed.
6. When staunch and steady to command on planted game birds, shoot all the birds with handler retrieving half of them. Insist dog remain at the place he found birds.
7. Finally shoot pigeons and one or more game birds every session and let dog retrieve most of them, but only on command.
8. Work dog in braces and teach dog to back (honor) bracemate.
9. Take dog hunting during open season and let him learn where to hunt and find native game, and have a ball while you are doing it!
10. Just for the record, Spot has now tripled in value over his original cost, including food, gasoline and training birds. But you probably would not sell him for five times this amount.

The first decision to be made by the prospective trainer, veteran or newcomer to the world of gun dogs is how he expects to use the dog when training is completed, as suggested in the chapter defining breed types. The end use will have a considerable bearing on the type

53

Introducing Natural Retrieving

The five photos on these two pages illustrate how to begin a routine of natural retrieving with a very young puppy. The trainer is Don Cranfill, his student is an eight-week-old Pointer puppy.

The action starts when the puppy is teased with the buck to arouse his interest. Following this, the buck is tossed a short distance where the puppy can see it. At the same time the puppy is given the command DEAD. After the buck is thrown the puppy is encouraged to go after it and bring it to the trainer. As the puppy delivers the buck to hand, he is commanded GIVE and is lavishly praised for his good performance.

of bird dog and perhaps on the breed of his choice. An experienced owner will know, but the new owner may need the counsel and advice he can get by reading good breed publications. He should certainly discuss it with friends who hunt with dogs and by visiting amateur and professional trainers.

If he lives in a state where pheasants provide the major bird crop—or if his bag is quail, woodcock or grouse—the game will have some influence on the decision because of the built-in normal hunting range of the dog he selects. As indicated earlier one can find a pointing dog breed almost tailor-made for the hunter who hunts the wide open spaces or the small restricted shooting preserves adjacent to a large city, and everything in between these two extremes. He should make every effort to select his puppy from a litter out of hunting parents of a hunting family. This precaution will not insure that he acquires a top prospect, but he can increase the odds of getting one if the parents and family have been good gun dogs.

Once the breed has been decided on and the individual eight- to ten-weeks-old puppy has arrived home, it is most important to visit the veterinarian for advice on shots. A new puppy will then be ready for his first early education.

If young Spot is to be a house dog, he should be house-broken. The method, slightly oversimplified, requires that he be taken out to the yard on a leash, the first thing in the morning, after each of his meals, several times in between and just before bedtime. Don't let him have the run of the house; keep him confined in a certain area. If he makes a mistake in the house clean it up and forget it unless you catch him in the act. In that case, a little tough scolding and making sure no one forgets about taking him out should bring results in a very short time. Be sure he is rewarded with kind words and much praise when he performs properly in the yard. Whether he is to be a kennel or house dog, the young puppy needs much attention—the animal behaviorists call it *socialization*. This means fraternizing with him several times daily in a way he enjoys . . . playing, romping.

After several days in his new home, teach him to lead by taking him for short walks on a light leather or nylon leash a few times daily. He may fight the leash at first but gentle treatment, coaxing and letting him do the guiding at first will overcome his fear. He will learn to like it after a time or two around the block. Once adjusted to his new home and recognizing his trainer as the source of food and kind treatment, he will form a lasting bond of affection with his owner-trainer. Teach him his name at this time by using it on all occasions.

The Basis of Obedience—Yard Training

The young bird dog should learn the basic and highly important commands early in life. When he approaches three months of age he should be ready for his first schooling in response to WHOA, STOP, COME, HEEL, and NO. One can teach them almost simultaneously, but a little time interval between them is recommended to avoid confusing him.

Begin these lessons by attaching the lead to the dog's collar and walking him in a secluded area—backyard, garage, basement—for a few minutes. Then give the command WHOA coupled with a short tug on the lead. Then hold it tight for a few seconds to force him to stand, not sit. Reward him with petting and kind words. Then give the command HEEL and resume walking. Force him to walk at heel with a tight lead. Repeat the routine of WHOA to stop and HEEL to move forward a dozen times during a ten to fifteen minute first training session. After two or three lessons he will be responding well to each command. Right-handed trainers usually teach the dog to work on their left side, or if left-handed on the opposite side, because most hunters carry the shotgun in the hand of their dominant side, which contributes to the dog's safety. A dog heeling at the left of his right-handed owner would then be safe from injury if the gun dropped or went off accidentally. After six training sessions, the young hopeful should learn to respond to WHOA and HEEL instantly with enjoyment. Training at this stage should not exceed more than ten to twenty minutes at a time. Short lessons prevent boredom and loss of interest by the average puppy with his short span of attention.

Teaching Response to Come

Teaching the dog to come when called is most important, and now is the time to lay the groundwork for this essential obedience. A quick and painless method for the novice trainer is to attach a 25-foot light nylon line, called a checkcord, to the dog's collar and work him for a minute or two on the WHOA and HEEL routines. Then pass the end of the checkcord behind a basement water pipe, a tree in the yard, or a stake in the ground. Holding the loose end of the cord in hand, give the command WHOA while walking away from the puppy. Tension on the line will keep him from following the trainer who should repeat the command WHOA several times as he walks away from the dog. The trainer should also accompany this action with his arm raised above his head. After a few seconds, he should give the command Spot, COME, after lowering his raised arm, and then spreading his hands palm out at his hips. A dozen five to ten minute sessions in which the routine is repeated will teach the youngster the command and the required response. Rewarding with petting and kind words for proper response will speed up the learning process. However, if young Spot is reluctant to come when called regardless of trainer's rewards and enticement, a bit of muscle can be added to the routine by passing the checkcord around a pipe, tree or stake and tying both ends of the checkcord to the dog's collar. Trainer can then not only enforce the command to WHOA by restraint on part of the checkcord, but also make the dog come to him by pulling on the other end. Once the pupil is responding to WHOA and Spot, COME, keep him at WHOA for increasingly longer periods up to five minutes, while walking around him in a wide circle.

By six months of age the puppy should respond to all three commands—WHOA, HEEL, and COME. He should perform well without leash or checkcord attached to his collar. If his response is not near-perfect to any one command, continue training with and without the leash until he *is* near-perfect.

Never nag a young dog; both dog and trainer must enjoy the session. Losing one's temper and roughing him up can cause the dog to perform sullenly or not at all. If this occurs stop the training immediately and put Spot back in the kennel or house for a week before resuming training sessions.

The last of the basic commands which the puppy should know by the time he is six months old are NO and KENNEL UP. NO should be the last command taught because of its negative effect. NO simply tells the dog to stop what he is doing. It is a highly useful tool in a thousand instances throughout the dog's life both in the field and in the house. Many puppies learn its meaning fast if the trainer gives it a stern voice. If Spot has a mind of his own about jumping out of the automobile before he is called, or in rushing up to a strange dog, he will soon get the message if firm, frequent NOs are accompanied by a swat over the rump with a leash or by physically restraining him. A daily refresher of this command can be given at feeding time by placing the feed pan before him and insisting that he wait a few seconds to eat. He will soon learn to respond to NO and wait for the signal O.K. Spot. Repetition and persistence pay off here as in every other training routine.

Teaching the Puppy to Enter an Enclosure

All hunting dogs must learn on command to enter an enclosure like an automobile, kennel box, hunting crate or room. Either of two commands, LOAD UP or KENNEL UP, may be used. Start your puppy by gently pushing him into a crate, kennel run or other enclosure when the command is given. Force him to remain there a few seconds. Then give the command Spot COME or Spot HEEL and reward him for correct performance. Repeat this routine a half dozen times each day until he learns what is required, gradually increasing the time he spends in the crate. If the command is used each time he is taken for a ride or at feeding time he will soon learn that he must always comply.

Arousing Pointing Instinct

Pointing dogs instinctively freeze into a rigid point on game or simulated objects which resemble game. This has been well documented by practical and scientific students of pointing dog behavior. Several theories are advanced to explain it, but the instinct to point is present in all the pointing dog breeds and some other breeds too, in varying degrees. A late German scientist of renown supports the opinion of many pointing dog trainers that it is well to arouse and intensify all the desirable instincts at an early age. The three-month-old prospect should be exposed to a routine, along with his yard work, which will in most cases arouse and demonstrate his instinct to point.

Sight-Pointing a Bird Wing

Tie a pigeon or quail wing to 15 feet of fishing line fixed to a casting rod. Flip the wing close to the puppy as he moves around the yard. Perhaps he has stiffened up in the kennel or yard when he has seen a butterfly, a grasshopper or a song bird. When he first sees the flipping wing, he will probably sight-point it for a second or two before diving in to catch it. Or it may take a few minutes of flipping the wing from ground to air and back before he attempts to point it. No commands should be given the youngster when he points. Such training should not be continued for more than a dozen short sessions, because young Spot is operating with his eyes which is not to be encouraged. To become a satisfactory hunting dog he will have to find game with his nose. Sight-hunting is not a desirable trait in a bird dog.

First Trips Afield

As already suggested, it is difficult to work up an exact time sequence for training a gun dog. The training schedule outlined in this book will give the novice trainer a general idea of how and when to start.

A pointing dog five months of age is not too young to go to a field containing some species of upland game for his first exposure to hunting. Begin by whoaing dog and holding for a few seconds as you elevate his tail, and then release with two blasts of the whistle. At first he won't know what it is all about. But he will soon learn to move out fast from his handler and check out all the strange new scents his nose tells him are around him. The field should be a half mile or so from a highway as scores of young dogs are killed or injured each year by traffic. It helps if there is a farm pond nearby where he can get a drink if he needs it. To be sure, you can carry a supply of water for the dog with you. In this first half-hour run he may strike game scent and telegraph it by his excitement and animation.

If it's early morning or late evening with birds holding tight on the roost, his clumsy puppy tactics might not disturb the game and he could whip into a flash point—before he jumps in and flushes. Naturally he will chase the airborne bird or running rabbit. That's good! The experience will increase his hunting desire and speed as he moves through the cover trying to find more of those tantalizing creatures. If he does not strike game on the first trip, he should do so on his second or third, and his hunting range should also increase. End the session while he is still at the peak of his enjoyment and before he tires.

In early trips afield the trainer will have an opportunity to test the effectiveness of yard training. Spot may not be ready to quit and

A three-month-old Pointer puppy, owned by the author, sight-pointing a pigeon wing.

A ten-week-old English Setter puppy, pointing a liberated Bobwhite by scent only. The puppy, owned by Wendell Womack, could not see the bird as he pointed it.

Goodall

may have a memory lapse on the commands WHOA and COME. In this case, continue the yard work at home and use it occasionally in the field while the dog hunts.

The trainer will know that early yard work was well learned when he can WHOA his puppy for two seconds when he is 50 or 100 yards away before sending him on with a wave of his hand and two short toots of the whistle. The half-hour sessions may be gradually increased to one hour by the time the youngster is nine months old, but not during hot weather except in early morning or late evening or if drinking water is available to the dog.

Bird Dog Retrieving

Any experienced hunting man will agree that the complete upland game hunting dog should be a good retriever for two reasons. First, a good retriever is a strong contributor to game conservation because he will collect 95% of the game which falls to the hunter's gun. Second, when he finds game for the gun and then collects it, he has done a complete job which is gratifying to his pleased owner, and often to the dog too.

But there is a wide difference of opinion among bird dog trainers as to when and how retrieving should be taught. Many knowledgeable pointing dog trainers, who perhaps represent the majority opinion, believe that it is much more difficult to train a dog to hold a point for an indefinite period if he has been conditioned to retrieve before becoming staunch. In most cases this means waiting until the dog is approaching two years of age and has become so dependable that he will hold point indefinitely. This may mean he will have to be force trained to fetch to become a good retriever.

The usual methods of force training are *not recommended* for the novice. Once force training is begun it must be followed through to the bitter end, and some people do not have the temperament to apply the unpleasant force nor some dogs to receive it. The traditional procedure is to place the dog on a table or chair and force a retrieving buck in his mouth while repeating the command FETCH or DEAD. In most cases he will refuse the buck or spit it out immediately so the trainer applies manual pressure to an ear or leg until the dog finally opens his mouth to avoid the pain. With more pressure he will learn to hold the buck when it is put in his mouth. The next step is to apply pressure to the now sore ear until the dog reaches for the buck which is held some six or eight inches away.

This lesson is repeated with the buck being gradually lowered until the dog will pick it up from a position at his feet when command is given and pressure applied. Finally, it is thrown eight or ten yards away from the dog with checkcord attached to his collar to prevent his departing this unpleasant "school room." Pressure is again applied until he will walk or run to the thrown buck and retrieve it to hand. We suggest using a combination of natural retrieving and one called OBEDIENCE RETRIEVING, for lack of a better name. It is guaranteed to make the dog a better retriever because he will enjoy the lessons while learning that he must retrieve objects his trainer orders him to collect under all circumstances.

By long time tradition, it has been a common practice of pointing dog professional trainers to force train pointing dogs to retrieve after they have become staunch and steady to wing and shot. They thought the staunching and steadying were much easier if the dog had not learned to retrieve. We changed our minds about force training when we saw a few dogs develop undesirable characteristics after such practice. Animal behaviorists from Cornell University suggested that force training could cause behavior problems. After much thought, we concluded that if it was not necessary to apply extreme pressure on a dog to teach him to sit, whoa, come or heel, it might not be necessary to apply pressure to make that dog a dependable retriever. In discussing the matter with a number of other people, one of whom was Ernest Wunderlich, it became our opinion that it will work with normal dogs which have not been spoiled or conditioned by fear to dislike retrieving. However, we know that many people believe forced retrieving is necessary to make a dependable retriever, so we will outline with descriptive photos a system of forced retrieving which is not as severe as some systems in common usage.

OBEDIENCE RETRIEVING was evolved by Ernest Wunderlich, a long time amateur trainer, of Joliet, Illinois. His collection of more than a hundred field trial trophies, and many thousands of limits of game birds retrieved by his dogs, qualify him as an authority on teaching dogs to retrieve. One begins training a puppy two or three months old with a rolled-up, knotted dishtowel which is tossed a distance of a few feet in the yard or basement for the puppy to retrieve several times a day. If Spot wants to be chased, a light cord attached to his collar will convince him rapidly that it's better to bring the object to hand and receive generous praise and petting than to bury it under some leaves. As his eyesight improves the dish

Teaching Forced Retrieving

Don Cranfill places the buck in the dog's mouth and teaches him to hold.

Pressure applied to the dog's ear will result in desired response.

The application of force coupled with the command FETCH will cause the dog to reach for the buck with its mouth open.

Next the dog must learn to reach down for the buck on command when force is applied to the ear.

The dog has now learned to pick up the buck on command with the use of force.

Here the dog picks up the buck in cover on force command.

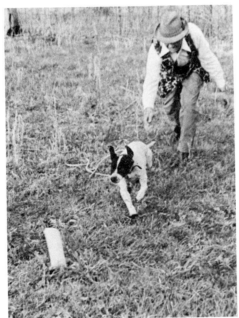

He next learns to fetch the buck which has been thrown a short distance.

The finished product of forced retrieving is a dog that will retrieve to hand on command and will hold its head up to deliver its bird and receive its reward.

towel can be replaced with a small canvas—never plastic—boat bumper and the distance of the retrieves increased gradually to 30 or more yards. It will increase Spot's youthful enthusiasm for the game if he is permitted to chase after the thrown buck. And it will be early training for the gun if the handler gives a sharp hand clap each time it is thrown. With continuous correct performance the dog is switched from a training buck to dead birds and/or feathered buck described in this section. Five minute daily training sessions in the yard with the dog completing 8 or 10 retrieves will teach him retrieving in the yard is a fun game which he will learn to enjoy.

The Hard-Feathered Retrieving Buck

The hard-feathered, retrieving buck or dummy serves the dual purpose of introducing the young dog to the feel and scent of feathers and encouraging him to fetch objects with a firm but gentle grip. This tool is constructed by rounding off the sharp edges of a twelve inch length of a 2 by 2 board and having the local tinsmith attach a permanent light metal sleeve around it. Finally, bird wings—of pigeon, quail, pheasant or duck—are attached by rubber bands or braided fishing line until they cover the metal sleeve. This tool and a larger size canvas boat bumper are now used intermittently in each retrieving lesson. The large size boat bumper will teach Spot to open his mouth wide enough to pick up a pheasant or a grouse. The hard buck will teach him to just grip the object firmly enough to hold it without biting down. Dogs do not like to bite down on metal, and this will help him learn to collect shot game with a tender mouth after his mouth becomes thoroughly conditioned by many yard retrieves.

Obedience Retrieving

At some period in his young life Spot must learn that retrieving is a serious business and he must always follow orders to do so. Once force training has been started, the trainer must continue through to the end or the dog may never retrieve again. Substituting a key ring or shotgun hull or household tool for the buck is a good way to start. Perhaps he will collect it at once, but then again maybe he won't. If he refuses, now is the time to begin the process of teaching him to be non-selective and highly obedient when ordered to retrieve. Rolling the new object in one's hands, or holding it in an armpit long enough to gather the trainer's scent, and then tossing it out, may be helpful

Heidi, a German Shorthaired Pointer, delivers a Chukar Partridge to professional trainer Steve Studnicki during a shoot at his private hunting club. *John Seyman*

Bill Goady's classy English Setter Misty delivering a harvested bird to hand.

for a time or two perhaps. But eventually the dog will refuse it. When this occurs the handler should pick up the object and place it gently in the dog's mouth and praise and pet him while holding it there by hand for ten seconds. Use the command GIVE to signal release, and lay on plenty of praise and petting. If he is reluctant to retain the object in his mouth, chuck him under the chin. Repeat this several times. Next, ask the dog to make a retrieve after a five-yard throw. Move backward while repeating words of praise. The dog may pick it up and come to heel the first time. Continue the routine three or four times, then knock off for that session. Repeat this procedure for a few minutes each day before or after the early yard work. It's a good change of pace and will help keep the puppy interested in both operations. Continue to introduce new objects into the early retrieving session and gradually convince the young dog by firm orders to fetch, with high praise for completion. This technique requires a gradual and continuing increase in firmness until the dog learns that he must comply. It is far easier to do than describe. Perhaps it can be summed up by saying that the trainer is using a slow, gradual method of imposing his will on the dog over a period of days by firmness and reward. The dog must not be intimidated by physical force. He must have respect—not fear—and carry out the retrieving with a merry tail and boldness. Dogs exposed to OBEDIENCE RETRIEVING have been known to seize a chair rung or table leg—even a prized antique—when ordered to do so.

Introducing Liberated or Planted
Birds Into The Training Routine

The use of liberated or hand-planted birds is a giant step forward for today's trainers for two reasons. First, it gives the trainer far better control of the situation when the young dog is in the presence of game. Second, it can speed up the time interval in teaching a young dog how to behave in the presence of game. It is also possible to correct—at a time and place of the handler's choosing—a fault which an older dog has developed. But the use of planted game has its limitation and should be used only to get the young pointing dog started correctly in pointing, holding the point, and being steady to wing and shot when birds are flushed. It can never contribute much to the development of bird sense. Only repeated exposure to native (wild) game will teach him to look for birds where they should normally be found and contribute to

Ted Mertes pushes the head of a dizzied pheasant under one wing before tucking the bird into the cover.

Champion Fidler's Pride, winner of the U.S. 1985 Open Chicken Championship and one day later handled again by Freddie Rayl to the International Quail Championship. Owned by Dan and Marge Bonaguidi, Pride's remarkable record includes 19 wins and placements.

development of the confident, hunting independence all good bird dogs must possess. Even though the use of planted birds is highly recommended as a training tool, the trainer should not expect that alone to produce a finished hunting dog.

When the young prospect is taken to the field get him in contact with native birds the first time or two. It will charge up his interest and arouse his desire to hunt and find game. But also expose him to planted birds. The human scent clinging to them through handling is not as attractive to the dog as the scent of native game. The eager youngster needs some wild birds to excite him and planted birds to teach him that they too can be fun.

Several different birds can be used in the training routine. Perhaps the most popular with trainers of pointing dogs, retrievers and spaniels is the rock dove. Don't let that name fool you. A rock dove is none other than the common pigeon seen roosting in a thousand barns, church steeples, tall buildings and even in palm trees of Southern California. Its great appeal is its ruggedness and easy care. If you start with a dozen or two Homers they will return after use to the holding place for food and water. So start with pigeons. Then switch to Bobwhite quail, Chukar partridge or pheasant. All three species of these upland game birds are raised in great quantity on many game farms. Check for suppliers in classified ads of outdoor magazines.

Pigeons may be planted by gripping the center of the body firmly and twirling in fast circles, causing the head of the bird to revolve rapidly fifteen or twenty times. The bird is then placed in a "nest" made by depressing cover the size of one's foot. Or pigeons may be carried in one's pocket and "dizzied" as described above, then rolled in (thrown into cover) behind the dog. Quail and Chukar may be planted the same way but gentler handling is necessary because they can't stand as much rough treatment. With large Chukar and pheasant the simplest way to "plant" them is to tuck the head under a wing; then with a two-handed grip around depressed wings, whirl the bird ten or twenty times and place it on its side where the head is tucked under in a stamped out nest in the cover. If the birds are not to be shot, attach a long string with one end tied to a coke bottle and the other to the leg of the planted bird (Chukar, pheasant or pigeon). This restricts the flush to a short distance and enables the handler to catch the bird when the training session is finished. A forty-foot white string will restrict a Bobwhite quail to a short flush for easy location.

If the young dog finds and chases a covey or two of quail—or attempts to outrun native pheasant he flushes by accident or design—it is time to roll in a dizzied pigeon behind him. The pigeon will remain there for perhaps five minutes. With practice a handler will learn how to keep a bird down for fifteen minutes or longer. By two or three changes in the direction he is walking, the trainer can guide the dog without much handling to the downwind side of the pigeon. Spot may flash point for a second or two and attempt to catch the bird. That's good and will be super good after he has found with his nose, flash pointed and chased both native and planted game a half dozen times on each of five to ten or more trips to the field. Perhaps Spot will be holding those flash points for five to ten seconds by the time he reaches nine or ten months of age. If he is to be a hunting dog, it's time to teach him to hold a point indefinitely and not for just a few seconds.

Teaching Pointing Dogs to Hold Point Staunchly

When exposed to enough liberated or native birds some young pointing dogs will learn to hold point almost automatically or at least respond to voice command to WHOA. Others may require a forceful lesson to learn that they must stop flushing birds and become staunch (hold point indefinitely). If hunted with dragging checkcord a dog can be corrected during the next several months when he forgets. Field trial prospects are often permitted to flush game through their derby year or two years old, but bird dogs used solely for hunting are often "staunched up" when they reach the age of a year or a year and a half. The long checkcord attached to the prospect's collar with a good harness snap is a highly useful training tool for staunching. Planted birds may be used to excellent advantage at this time.

The action begins when the trainer plants a pigeon very tight by one of the methods suggested earlier. The cover should be high enough so the dog must use his nose, and not his eyes, to find it. The dog must not see the bird planted.

The handler then starts the dog downwind from the hidden pigeon and hunts him towards the bird while repeating the command CAREFUL, Spot—BIRDS HERE. When Spot strikes body scent of the planted bird and flash points, handler immediately takes up the slack in checkcord and holds the dog firmly while repeating command WHOA quietly and firmly. Loud shouting is not advisable at this time: it may confuse the dog. Loud commands should be saved for emergency conditions. Handler should hand-walk the tight checkcord slowly. When he reaches the dog he should squat down at the dog's rear and gently push the dog's body towards the bird. Spot will lean back usually as the handler continues to repeat softly WHOA—Spot—WHOA—GOOD BOY. As the dog holds his point in an acceptable manner, the handler can gently rub the full length of the dog's tail upward against the hair, lifting it slowly to a higher position.

If Spot attempts to flush the pigeon after a three-second flash point despite the tight restraint of the checkcord, the handler should lead him away from the bird forcibly, stop some distance away and calm the excited dog with petting and soft talk. He can then hunt Spot in an area without game and refresh the dog's memory on WHOA a half dozen times, requiring the dog to remain standing for two to three minutes at a time with vocal command and checkcord.

The dog must be letter perfect in the dry-run routine on vocal command to WHOA. If he does not respond perfectly with no bird scent in his nose, he certainly will not respond when he does smell game. Perfect response is the clue that he is ready for another session with a planted bird. Perhaps this time the restraint on the checkcord, coupled with soft voice commands to WHOA, will induce the dog to extend his point long enough for the handler to hand-walk the tight checkcord to the dog. He can then apply pressure on the dog's hips and force him gently towards the bird. The dog should not only hold but will lean back against the pressure and continue to point staunchly. If Spot is slightly bull-headed or if the handler is lax in teaching the command WHOA, the exercise should be repeated and thoroughly this time.

Some trainers take a short cut by using a spiked training collar that pinches a dog's neck when the checkord is tightened. They let the dog flush and run the full length of the fifty foot checkcord then dump him hard with a spiked or choke collar. It may be a faster method but can start Spot on the way to becoming a blinker. Blinking, the worst fault a bird dog can have, means the dog responds to game scent by shying away from it, going in the opposite direction or at best exhibits an uncertain or fearful attitude when he scents game. Constant application of too much pressure reinforces such undesirable conduct. Repetitious training routines with mild rewards and gentler punishment, and not harsh or severe force,

The Pigeon Pole

A "pigeon pole" is a handy device to teach a pointing dog to hold point staunchly. It is also used to teach steadiness to flush. The pictures on these two pages will show some of the techniques of training with the pigeon pole.

The young trainee is brought up to the tied pigeon (off camera) and forcibly prevented from attempting to flush by the use of a tight check cord and the command WHOA.

Top: After several sessions the dog will sight point the pigeon with less restraint. Note handler pushing the dog gently toward the bird to encourage staunchness. *Center:* As training continues, so does staunchness. The trainer continues to stroke the dog's tail and encourage him verbally. This dog will soon be firmly convinced he is not to flush birds at any time. At that time the handler can begin steadying the dog to flush. *Bottom:* Early training in steadying the dog to flush can be resumed at the pigeon pole. The trainer nudged the pigeon into a short flight while commanding the dog WHOA. When the dog is staunch on point and steady to flush in the yard, he can be tried on liberated birds which he will find and point a distance from the handler.

Southern Regional Bird Hunters Champion Dust Buster owned by Tom Mofield and handled by Randy Payne, stands high and tight as he smokes a covey of Bobwhite Quail.

Harley Fancher with two time winner of Arkansas Amateur Shooting Dog of the Year, HOSS FLY. Fancher and wife Diann produced 29 of 31 English Setters which have won Dog of the Year awards.

produce an animated, happy performer which loves all phases of the work.

A fine and highly successful British trainer with more than 3000 trained gun dogs—pointing dogs, spaniels and retrievers—to his credit says, "You can beat a lot out of a dog, but you can't beat anything into him." An animal behaviorist from Cornell University provides the scientific basis for this philosophy by stating that every ounce of excess force used in getting a dog to respond will show up elsewhere in his behavior pattern—often in an undesirable manner. Excessive force when the dog is in the presence of game often produces a blinker or runaway bolter, or a perpetual heeler which won't hunt. Unfortunately, we have seen all three kinds.

When the dog is staunch for two to three minutes on his first bird, the trainer should have a friend flush the bird and fire a 32 blank pistol as the dog chases it with checkcord attached. This action must be repeated until the dog will hold point on pigeons and planted game staunchly.

Steadying to Flush and Shot

By the age of 16 to 18 months, a dog should be staunch on pigeons and some game birds. He should hold point for, possibly, up to five minutes 40 or 50 times without undesirable behavior. He must not circle the game, let down when the handler approaches, repeatedly turn his head to observe the handler, lower his tail between his legs, or show other indications of fear, confusion or unhappiness. He will then be ready for steadying to flush and shot if he is hunting well and responding to all commands. Being steady simply means he will stay on point when game is flushed and until ordered to retrieve or resume hunting. Most hunting dogs are staunch on point but are not trained to be steady to flush and shot and will give chase after the handler flushes game or game lifts for any reason.

The advantages of having a steady dog are many. One, especially in pheasant country, he won't run over and flush other game. Neither will he chase a covey or single bird over a highway, or over a steep bluff. We have seen two fine dogs killed in a fall over a bluff while chasing. And we know of a number killed by highway traffic a half mile or more away from the owner. Finally, the steady-to-flush-and-shot dog is under control at all times. He should display this control even when braced with another dog which is not steady. Amateur Shooting Dog or Shoot-to-Kill field trial stakes usually require steadiness.

Training the young dog to be steady is similar to teaching him to be staunch. First restrain him with checkcord and command WHOA while a friend flushes the bird and fires a blank pistol or shot gun. Two or three sessions in the field where the dog is forced to be steady to flush will give him the idea. The handler can reinforce the commands by standing in front of the dog with arm raised overhead as the bird is flushed by the friend. When the dog holds, the friend can kill a pigeon, but the dog must NOT retrieve until he receives the command of Spot, DEAD or Spot, FETCH. His name should always be used as a part of the command so he will know the retrieve is his when working with a steady bracemate. Name use helps in field trials for control of your dog even if the bracemate is not steady. A trainer working by himself in the early stages of steadying can WHOA his dog at heel, step on the checkcord, and fly a pigeon to be shot for the dog's retrievel ONLY on command.

A good procedure is to work the dog on six birds, three of which he retrieves. The handler walks out to retrieve the other three with the dog required to remain WHOAd at point where the bird is released. When the dog exhibits rock-steadiness in two or three sessions with a couple of dozen pigeons shot for him, the handler can switch the routine to letting the dog hunt, find and point birds while dragging the checkcord. When point is established, the handler should walk carefully past the dog, giving soft WHOA commands repeatedly. He should then flush the bird and shoot it, being careful to caution the dog before and after shot with the command WHOA or STAY. This procedure should give a clear indication that the dog understands and enjoys the work, has absorbed the disciplined training, and willingly performs all of it as the owner desires. If the dog breaks flush or shot, try to prevent his retrieving and drag him back to the spot where he broke. Then swat his rear with the lead while scolding him. Continue light punishment whenever he breaks until he responds correctly every time. Do reward him generously when he responds correctly. See pigeon pole technique photos for other methods of teaching staunchness and steadiness to flush and shot.

Honoring a Pointing Brace Mate by Backing

Training Spot to honor another dog's point by backing—actually pointing the other dog—comes last because it may be difficult for the one-dog man to find the opportunity to work with another dog. But Spot must learn to back because point stealing is a serious fault and may lead to birds flushed out of range, dog fights and other undesirable actions. Some pointing dogs have a natural tendency to back while others must be trained.

Begin the procedure by requesting a friend with a dog which is 100% staunch to have his dog point a tightly planted pigeon or game bird. Then lead Spot up behind the older dog and force him to WHOA by command and restraint on the checkcord. When he responds repeat the steadying technique and push him gently toward the pointing dog. If he tries to move forward, sharp jerks on the checkcord and vocal commands to WHOA will get the message over. Much repetition will be necessary to make him a dependable backer. If the backing time is gradually increased in each training session, Spot should be considered dependable when he backs for five minutes after a dozen or two exposures. In the last few sessions the planted bird should be flushed and shot. If Spot is backing without restraint or vocal command, the older dog should be sent to retrieve.

Measure Progress. Finish by Actual Hunting.

A progress report from the handler to himself at this stage will reveal that he has a bird dog one-and-a-half-years-old which responds instantly to the verbal commands and hand signals of WHOA—STAY—COME—HEEL—and moves out to hunt, always on two short whistle blasts. The dog also hunts and finds domestic pigeons and released quail or pheasant with good desire and intensity. He backs or holds point for an indefinite time, and remains styled-up staunch after the bird is flushed—or will remain at least motionless after the handler flushes and shoots the bird. The dog retrieves only on specific command. This stage of development represents the basic education the gun dog prospect must have. It is now up to his owner-trainer to give him practical hunting experience

Teaching to Back

In this series of photos trainer Don Cranfill teaches a young dog to back by taking it out with more experienced kennel mates. The trainer has planted a bird tightly in the cover and released an older, staunch dog to point it. He then leads the trainee to area, commanding him to WHOA and restraining him with the check cord.

Still using the WHOA command and stepping on the check cord for additional control, the trainer pushes the dog forward as in earlier training for staunchness and strokes the tail to style up the point.

The trainer continues the same teaching methods described in the upper photo until the dog learns he must honor another dog's point staunchly just as he must with a bird.

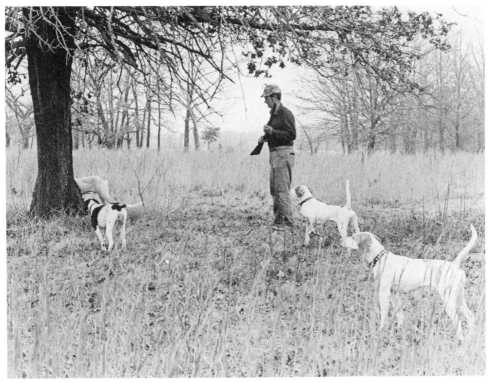

The liver and white Pointer at the left has progressed to the point of working without the check cord. His tail held out behind him shows that he is still not quite sure of himself. Working with other dogs will help develop a dog's confidence and dependability. It generally requires several sessions with two or more dogs in the action to achieve the desired degree of perfection.

Dog training is learned early in Arkansas. Here ten-year-old Wayne Dockings cautions the derby-winning Pointer Leisa not to break as his dad flushes a planted quail. *Goodall*

The author with Herb Holmes (right). Holmes, owner of Gunsmoke Kennels, is one of America's outstanding amateur trainers and handlers. He has bred many fine pointing dogs and is a member of the Field Trial Hall of Fame.

Dodson

for developing the bird sense to learn where the birds are normally found (not often on a totally bare or plowed field) and how to handle the regular and the unusual behavior of native (wild) game birds. They, too, have a certain degree of intelligence and take every opportunity to throw a curve at Spot when he is searching for them in cover. Birds change direction while running, hide in cover, and then flush after Spot and his master have passed them. There is no substitute for experience on wild game. The more of it the dog gets the better he will be as a bird finder and hunting companion.

The German Shorthaired Pointer, Dual Ch. Fritz Von Der Zigeuner, owned by John A. Marksz, also holds an amateur field championship in Canada and is an obedience degree winner. To his many accomplishments in competition, Fritz is his owner's personal shooting dog. Like the Brittany, the German Shorthair often functions as a dual dog. In their wisdom, the framers of both breeds' Standards achieved as a model of perfection a show dog that could also perform commendably in the hunting field.

Gun dog Springer Highland Jimmy and owner Walley Crawford. Jimmy is about to be cast into a millet field loaded with Pheasant and Mourning Doves.

Mrs. Leonard (Kay) Aldridge with two of her good Springer gun dogs. Mrs. Aldridge has handled her Sea of Saighton with success in national open competition. She is an example of many women handlers who achieve success with Springers. The Springer's desire to please and the softer touch of a woman often make for a strong winning combination.

Bud Daley

6

How to Train Spaniels

THE QUESTIONS MOST OFTEN asked about gun dog training are when and how to start, and what the various training routines are. The suggested time sequence must often be modified by the factors of aptitude and mental development of the individual dog, seasonal climatic conditions and the owner's available time. The sequence is based on practical experience and is basically accurate. If the new trainer-owner's motivation is strong, he will find the right dog, the necessary time and the correct, personalized training technique, with some trial and error perhaps, to get the job done.

Here is the general outline of the training schedule for a spaniel:

Eight to Twelve Weeks of Age—Yard Work

1. Socialize the puppy with frequent play periods and short walks on the lead and collar. Teach the dog its name.
2. Begin early retrieving routine with knotted hand towel and hand claps.
3. Early lessons in HUP, COME, NO and STAY by voice and hand signals. Use no pressure.
4. Substitute the towel with the large canvas buck for retrieving. Use a cap pistol for first experience with gun shot.

Three to Six Months of Age

1. Continue yard work routines but require gradually more exacting response.
2. Substitute the hard buck for retrieving using a blank pistol.
3. Begin trips to the field and encourage puppy to find and chase game.
4. Teach the dog to KENNEL UP and remain in the car or the kennel.
5. Introduce to the water, if the air and water temperature is at least 50 degrees.
6. Introduce to planted pigeons—blank pistol fired as puppy chases them.
7. Steady puppy (no chase) to retrieving in the yard—retrieve only on command.
8. Continue routine for more response to hand, voice and whistle signals to HUP—STAY—COME—and turn while hunting.

Six to Nine Months of Age

1. Continue yard work twice weekly and require perfect response to all voice and whistle commands and hand signals.
2. Introduce to double land retrieves with soft and hard buck in the yard, then in the field. Always use come-in whistle and insist dog fetch only on command.
3. Begin retrieving dead, then live, clipped-wing pigeons after the discharge of blank pistol with dog steady at heel. Switch to shotgun if all goes well.
4. As he HUPS at heel, shoot live birds for the youngster to retrieve.
5. Begin double water retrieves with thrown birds after gun shot. Then finish off doubles with shot pigeons—dog required to be steady at heel.

Ten to Twelve Months of Age

1. Continue yard work twice a week in the field with both bucks and dead birds.
2. Begin steadying dog to flushed birds while hunting. Throw a few dead birds, then live pigeons over his head while hunting. If all goes well, shoot live, planted pigeons.
3. Introduce to trailing moving game.
4. Work dog in brace with another spaniel, if yours is now working

well. Discourage at once any trailing, tagging-on (following the other dog) or playing. Handlers on parallel course 70 yards apart.

Twelve to Fifteen Months of Age

1. Weekly refresher of yard work or in field using all obedience and retrieving sequences with all commands.
2. Begin use of planted game birds (hen pheasants preferred). Spaniel to find, flush and retrieve with discipline and manner, showing ability to trail running birds and restraint to HUP when so ordered at long gun range.
3. Work dog dry (and with planted birds later) on crosswind and downwind course until acceptable pattern perfected.
4. Work occasionally on native game without shooting it—but discharge pistol!
5. Begin routine of working from blind, boat and through decoys, first with buck and then with shot pigeons.
6. Shoot some hand-thrown domestic mallards over water for the spaniel to retrieve.
7. Work the dog in the field in half-hour sessions with an occasional pigeon and game bird rolled in behind him. Expect him to be steady to wing and shot, much of the time automatically without command.
8. Concentrate on the dog learning the correct range of 35 to 40 yards to the side, and expect him to change direction much of the time without command.
9. Take the trained spaniel hunting on opening day and expect him to amaze his proud owner and shooting friend with his finish and polish. Pat yourself on the back for a job well done.

How to Train a Springer Spaniel Gun Dog

The education of a Springer gun dog—which is to be converted from a friendly, playful six- to eight-weeks-old puppy to a two-year-old obedient, trained bird-finder and retrieving specialist—can be a challenging and rewarding experience. It can be a lot of fun, too, because working and conditioning a live animal to use all his native ability to do exactly what you want him to do under any and all circumstances is far more satisfying than achieving mechanical skill with a golf club or tennis racket. There are no age barriers for the human who sets out on such a course of action. Many hunters approaching senior citizenship enjoy this fine recreational activity.

A dog that has been properly trained in obedience retrieving can usually be depended upon to retrieve enthusiastically in the field. These two photographs show the author's English Springer, Cripple Creek LeRoi. At left he has an empty shotgun shell and in the photo below he carries a roll of wrapping paper. As a result of his training he will fetch any object he can pick up and carry. *Goodall*

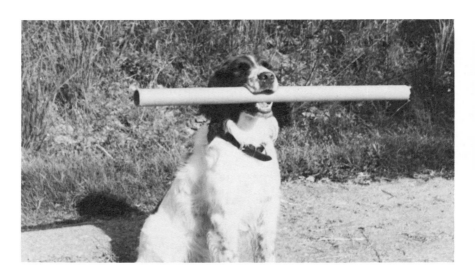

And the dog is not the only member of the team who learns—the trainer will expand his knowledge and experience as a hunter and outdoorsman by observing the behavior of the dog and the game. An ancient adage says that the best trainer is the one who has spoiled the most dogs. We prefer to reverse this slightly and say the best trainer is he who fits the training routine to the individual dog so as to produce a completely obedient animal whose inherited ability has been developed to its maximum potential and who performs joyfully with great spirit and animation.

Socializing the Young Prospect

Students of animal behavior who have done in-depth research with dogs, such as the late Clarence Pfaffenberger, have proven conclusively that socializing the new puppy is the first and most important step in the training process. And socializing simply means playing with the youngster several times each day, and taking him for walks on and off the leash or short rides in the car, to give him the confidence he needs when he has been removed from the security of his mother and litter mates. Dr. Michael Fox, an outstanding expert on animal behavior, contributes to this by saying that new puppies should not be taken away from the litter to a new home in the seventh week of life because of a physical change in their nervous system at this time. So it is recommended that the puppy be moved to his new home after the eighth week of his life and given much kind attention by his new owner and family as the first step in his education as a future gun dog.

Early Retrieving Exposure

English Springer Spaniels from field-bred stock have been blessed with a strong instinct to retrieve. This will often be shown by the youngster carrying objects during periods of play.

A rolled-up handkerchief or dish towel is a good object to use for a Springer's first retrieving lessons. If the object is dangled in front of his nose and then slowly tossed four or five feet, he will run to the object and snatch it up, then perhaps move away from the trainer. Calling his name and clapping one's hands while backing away from the puppy will usually persuade him to bring the object to hand. The action should be repeated four or five times, then discontinued while the young dog is at the peak of his enjoyment. Three or four such sessions each day for a week with the owner never—repeat never-chasing the dog but always cajoling him to bring it to hand is good for starters. The owner should shower the puppy with much petting and praise each time the object is retrieved to hand. If the youngster persists in moving away from the trainer, a light string can be attached to its collar and just enough pressure exerted to bring him to hand. Too much force at this point will cause the dog to drop the bundle and show decreasing interest in the game.

The next step is to exchange the rolled-up dish towel for a small canvas (not plastic) boat bumper and continue the lessons with this object. When the youngster is responding well, one can follow a plan suggested by a successful amateur trainer, Ernest Wunderlich of Joliet, Illinois. Mr. Wunderlich adds a key ring, empty shot gun hull, pocket knife or numerous other objects to the retrieving lessons which increase the variety of objects the youngster will retrieve. By the time he is six months old he should pick up anything the trainer points to at the command, Spot FETCH. Beginning with the first retrieving lessons with the canvas buck, add a sharp hand clap every time the buck is thrown until he becomes so conditioned that he will look for a falling object every time he hears a handclap.

Double Retrieves

The hand clapping is early training for the noise of a gun and is a sure way to prevent gun-shyness, which is a man-made fault in most cases. The next step is to exchange the small canvas buck for a larger one. At this time, introduce another retrieving buck made by attaching a metal sleeve around a 2 by 2 cut to 12 or 14 inch length with rounded corners. When pigeon, duck or pheasant wings are attached to the metal sleeve with rubber bands, this should be included in the daily retrieving lessons. If the youngster, now three or four months old, is reluctant at first to pick up the feathered buck, he can be teased repeatedly with it for a few seconds before it is thrown for a short distance. Eventually he learns to love it. The length of the retrieves should be increased as the puppy gets older from a few yards to 30 or 40 to teach him to mark the fall of distant objects. Longer retrieves, with some in weed field cover ten inches high, will teach the dog to mark longer falls accurately. The dog should always be given a series of five or six short toots of the whistle as a COME-IN signal.

When the spaniel is retrieving both the canvas and the metal covered bucks well, both can be thrown simultaneously. When he returns with the first one (usually the last one thrown) and has been praised, send him back for the second one, preceded by the command BACK and wave of arm in the proper direction. Trainer should not hesitate to walk out part way the first few times until Spot gets the idea that there are now two objects to fetch each time instead of one.

Some youngsters occasionally display a reluctance to release the retrieving buck, or to circle the handler, or even stand ten feet away instead of coming to heel. Start corrective action at once before such bad manners become a fixed habit. If the trainer insists firmly but gently that the dog come to heel with the buck and HUP immediately in front of the handler, such puppy-like behavior can be quickly nipped in the bud. If necessary use the light 15-foot checkcord described earlier. Too much force may cause him to drop the buck, but some gentle urging and petting will usually induce the puppy to pick it up again and come in with it. The command Spot FETCH can be helpful if the buck is dropped at handler's feet and not delivered to hand. The command COME or HEEL should be added to the routine and also three or four short chirps on the whistle, all of which are COME IN signals. If Spot is reluctant to release the buck at the command GIVE or OUT, he will soon learn to release if slight pressure is applied on his lower jaw forcing the skin against his lower teeth. One can also blow in his nose while repeating the command GIVE to encourage the dog to release.

The Framework of Complete and Total Obedience

The framework of total obedience, to which the dog must respond for the rest of his life, may be started at an early age. It consists of learning total and immediate response to five commands: HUP, STAY, COME, NO and KENNEL UP. The first lessons should begin when the puppy is three months of age. He will learn his name and to COME quickly if the command is given COME Spot every time he is fed. The scientific basis for this, according to some behaviorists, is that success followed by reward produces and reinforces similar behavior. Gratifying his hunger is the reinforcer, and if he is always called to the feed pan it will teach him to COME and make him anxious to comply.

To HUP

Teaching the young hopeful to HUP (sit) can be done in a few

Instant Response to HUP

In this series, trainer Dan Langhans, working with Andy Shoaff's trial winner Brian Picolo, demonstrates a highly useful technique for developing instant response to the HUP command.

As the trainer hups the dog he holds a concealed stick or fly rod tip behind his back.

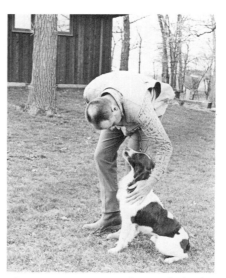

The trainer reassures and rewards the dog for the correct response.

As the dog walks at heel the trainer gives the voice or whistle command HUP, gently striking the dog at the same time. The dog is conditioned by surprise rather than pain.

five-minute training sessions by fixing a short, three-foot lead to his collar and leading him around the training area in a secluded spot away from other dogs, children and other distractions. He may fight the lead at first, but a little petting and coaxing will soon teach him to lead when given the command HEEL while on lead. The next step is to stop walking at frequent intervals. Then, giving the command HUP, lift his head gently with the lead and push down on his hips until he assumes the sitting position. Naturally he should be rewarded. He should learn the desired response in five or ten minutes but only be required to HUP for four or five seconds at first. One short, sharp blast of the whistle should also be used for HUP occasionally.

Sitting time may be gradually increased over a one to two week period. No force should be used except to push the dog into a sitting position when he occasionally fails to respond.

Puppies have a short span of attention and may decide in the middle of the training session that some other activity is more interesting. Consequently, several five-minute sessions each day are much more productive than one of 20 to 30 minutes. When Spot is older, if he "forgets" to HUP and switches to a standing position instead, there is a quick way to improve his memory. Handler with dog at heel should conceal a light flyrod tip against his off leg and simultaneously with the command HUP or one short blast of the whistle strike the dog's rump lightly with a backhand stroke. The dog does not see it but his reflexes will be conditioned by shock and surprise, and he will respond instantly. Repeat this lesson three or four times as required.

To STAY

When the puppy is responding well and HUPS instantly on whistle or voice command, the trainer can teach the command to STAY. One way to begin is to back away when the youngster is in the HUP position and with arm extended overhead—palms out—firmly command STAY or HUP. (Some trainers use the command HUP to also mean STAY until released. Others use HUP for sitting and STAY for remaining in that position.) If the puppy attempts to follow when handler moves out several steps, pick him up and return him to the original hupped position. Gentleness is the proper technique here as one is teaching and not forcing. A half-dozen times will usually teach the dog that he is to remain in a sitting position for five or ten seconds until handler walks back to praise him. Gradually the distance and time intervals are increased until the spaniel assumes the desired position for two or three minutes. When the handler can circle the sitting dog or back ten or more feet away without dog moving, the command has been learned. It's usually no problem in the seclusion of the training area to get the prospect to come when called from the HUP position. If it is a problem, attaching a lightweight checkcord to the collar and gently bringing the dog to heel will produce the required response. Alternate verbal command to COME with the whistle command in several short chirps. Also introduce hand signal to COME with hands at side, palms open.

Retrieve on Command

When the dog is five or six months old he should be responding to all the commands every time. He is now ready to learn to remain hupped at heel and to wait for the command FETCH before retrieving. Begin the lesson with the dog at heel (left heel for right-handed trainers) and toss the buck out a few feet, restraining the dog with the leash while repeating the command HUP or STAY several times. After five seconds give the command Spot FETCH and release him to retrieve. Two or three training sessions of five minutes each will usually convince him that he must wait for the command before he can retrieve. Keep the light checkcord attached to collar at first so that he can be corrected if he offers to retrieve before the command is given. The time interval and length of the retrieve should gradually be increased until the dog is completing 35-yard single and double retrieves in the yard under dependable control. A sharp hand clap or discharge of a cap pistol should be included in the routine on every work session.

Classroom sessions in obedience are not the only activity that the six-months-old puppy should be exposed to. He should have been taken to the field at five months and allowed to do pretty much as he pleases. He'll be excited by last night's stale rabbit scent, or chase a butterfly or lark and begin searching his first time out. If he spots a rabbit or game bird in the cover, he will probably chase it for a hundred feet, then return to the place he first saw it and sniff the wonderful new scent time and time again.

Now is the time to introduce a few "planted" pigeons for the youngster to find, flush and chase. Pigeons or game birds may be "planted" in a variety of ways. The simplest way for the new trainer is to hold the pigeon in one hand, whirl its body in short circles so the bird's head spins. Then tuck the head under one wing, and place the bird in a nest in the cover made by flattening out a place with one's foot. One can soon learn to plant pigeons which will remain in the cover for ten minutes or longer. This gives the trainer the opportunity to return to his car for the dog and work him upwind (wind blowing from bird to dog and trainer) to the bird. The spaniel becomes very excited when he scents the pigeon and moves in to investigate it. When it flushes he will chase it for some distance. When this occurs he should be well rewarded. Pigeons are usually available at a local poultry market or from a farm boy. It's necessary to introduce the youngster to them at an early age for several reasons. Most gun dogs when first exposed to quantities of native game may be reluctant to work pigeons later on. Also the use of planted birds speeds up training immeasurably because the trainer can set up in minutes any situation he desires instead of waiting hours or days to accomplish the same thing with native game. Pigeons are inexpensive and easy to handle and will reduce training expense to a minimum.

In planting game birds the trainer should make every effort to plant them so the youngster will not learn to follow his trail back to the birds. This is easily accomplished by walking upwind the distance the bird is to be planted, then moving 50 or more yards crosswind to a pre-determined area, then moving ten yards or so back downwind to plant the bird. Since the young dog should always be worked into the wind at this stage such procedure prevents him from trailing the foot scent of the planter to the bird (See diagram). After the young dog is hunting well and finding and chasing planted pigeons with enthusiasm, he will be ready to have a bird or two shot.

Shooting Game for a Spaniel Puppy

Earlier it was suggested that a sharp hand clap and the discharge of a cap pistol accompany every throw of the retrieving buck for conditioning the dog to look for something to retrieve every time he hears those sounds. The next step is to put the dog at heel and throw a cold, dead pigeon for him and simultaneously discharge a small caliber pistol. If no evidence of timidity is observed after a half-dozen shots, he is ready for the shot gun. Invite a friend to shoot live pigeons for you. Place the youngster at heel, then get his

Teaching Steadiness to the Thrown Buck

Trainer Dan Langhans makes wise use of a table for this phase of training. Working from a table conditions the dog to jump and makes breaking on the thrown buck more difficult than if the dog were on the ground.

To start, the dog is ordered to JUMP on the table. In the center photo, with the dog in a sitting position, the trainer places the buck in the dog's mouth. He taps the dog gently under the chin to encourage the trainee to keep holding the buck. As the buck is thrown, the trainer commands the dog to HUP or STAY.

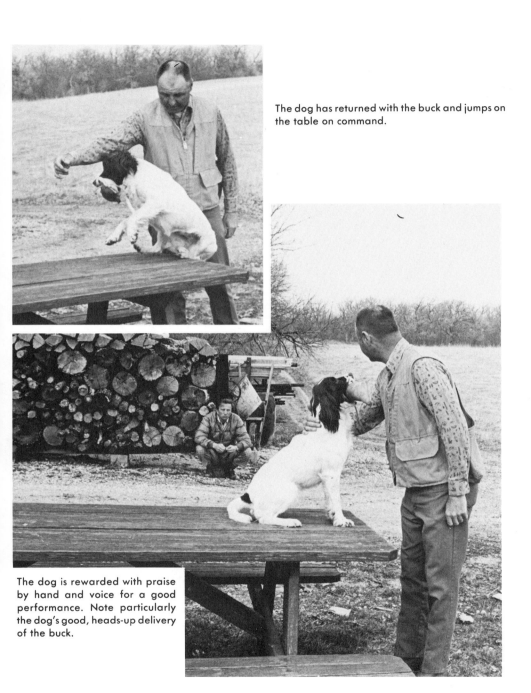

The dog has returned with the buck and jumps on the table on command.

The dog is rewarded with praise by hand and voice for a good performance. Note particularly the dog's good, heads-up delivery of the buck.

97

Encouraging the Springer's Natural Enthusiasm

The dog is being teased by the trainer with a live, clipped-wing pigeon.

The dog is encouraged to jump for the bird. This will lead to a pattern of bold flushes later.

As the trainer prepares to sail the bird away, the dog wheels sharply, prepared to chase.

The pigeon is sailed cross wind over the bare ground. At this point the dog takes off in hot pursuit since he has not yet been steadied to flush.

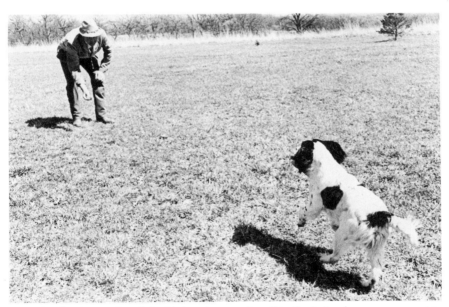

Here the dog has retrieved the bird and responds well to the trainer's encouragement to "hurry back."

When the dog returns to the trainer with the bird, the trainer gives the command HUP. This prepares the dog to deliver his bird and receive appropriate praise for a job well-done. Finally, as the handler reaches for the bird with his left hand he gives the dog his deserved praise with the right.

attention by having the friend call MARK while positioned some 40 or more yards to the front of the dog and handler. It's helpful to down the first bird for the dog to retrieve but a miss is not detrimental to training. If the early work was done properly no problems should arise.

If a problem occurs, start over with cap pistol in the yard, thrown dead birds, and so on. If all is well the gunner may gradually move to one side of the dog and handler, and continue to shoot several dozen birds to be retrieved during the next three or four training sessions. In every case the handler should insist that the spaniel remain hupped at heel until ordered to retrieve. At this point Spot should be letter perfect on steadiness, and will be if this work was done as described. If he breaks (leaves before command FETCH) bring him back to the spot and punish him. The youngster is ready for the next step which is finding, flushing and retrieving planted game which will be shot, providing he has not offered to break on thrown or shot birds for the last two dozen times.

Young dogs should not only be prevented from learning to trail the bird planter. They should also never see a bird being planted. So confine your dog in a small kennel box or solid crate while in the field when not actually working.

Spot has now demonstrated rock steadiness to thrown, shot birds while at heel, and is approaching twelve months of age. Begin the next step by throwing first dead and then live birds over his head while he hunts and quarters, preceded by shotgun or pistol shot. Repeat this until he responds to whistle, voice or arm signal to HUP—then let him flush planted pigeons. The voice or whistle commands to HUP should *not* be given until the moment the bird becomes airborne and as a warning again after the bird is shot. He'll probably be steady to flush and shot on the first two or three efforts, then break shot next time. Trainer should prevent retrieve, if possible, and indicate his displeasure vocally as he carries the dog back to point of flush. After three or four birds have been properly handled, the routine should be concluded for that day. Constant repetition will eventually cause the dog to become dependably steady, but the trainer must insist on correct performances.

Eventually the spaniel will learn to drop or HUP automatically (without command) to flush and shot. This routine should be continued at each training session for several weeks until the dog is letter perfect in finding, flushing and retrieving. He should be required to show good manners in retrieving by fast pick-up and

Introduction to Live Birds

The Springer in these four photos has been trained to be steady to a thrown buck or thrown, dead birds in yard and open field. He is now given thrown, *live* pigeons while questing. The trainer, R. S. Renick, prepares to sail the pigeon before the quartering dog.

While the pigeon is airborne the trainer HUPS the dog with one whistle blast and a raised arm signal.

102

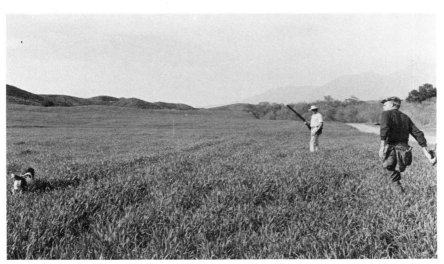

The dog has responded to the HUP command and is intently watching the bird.

The trainer cautions the dog to remain in position as gunner Dick Lane prepares to drop the bird.

Rolling In Dizzied Game

R. S. Renick demonstrates the correct technique for rolling in a slightly dizzied pheasant behind his questing Springer (not in photo).

The handler gives whistle and hand signal command to HUP after the dog was called in to flush the bird.

The dog is alertly marking the bird's flight while the handler cautions him to hold his position with a whistle and raised arm signal. Gunner Clark Hughes takes aim on the pheasant which has flown out of camera range.

104

quick return to the handler's feet, where he should sit before delivering the bird. If the youngster gives chase occasionally, he should then be picked up and carried back to point of flush and scolded verbally with perhaps a swat or two with hand, and verbal or whistle commands to HUP—HUP—HUP are repeated firmly. If breaking flush or shot persists, the handler can return to the earlier lesson with dog required to sit restrained at heel as handler steps on leash when birds are thrown and pistol is discharged. Or he may attach a 20-yard checkcord to the dog's collar and physically restrain him from breaking when the planted bird is flushed. The checkcord is not a good tool in the hands of a novice trainer and, if used, the dog should only be restrained and never jerked.

Quartering and Turning on Whistle Signal

Quartering the hunting areas, a necessary basic in a flushing dog, might be simply defined as a back and forth, effective hunting pattern similar to the action of windshield wipers on a car. Some young spaniels appear to have almost a built-in desire to quarter. Others need little and some much exposure to acquire it. If the earlier lesson of always working the dog into the wind (wind blowing into the face of the dog and the handler) is followed, most young spaniels will quarter back and forth almost automatically, turning outside away from the handler upwind at the end of each sideward cast. But the turn should be a complete, sharp 90 degree reversal of direction so that the dog will cross a few yards in front of handler as he continues his cast to the other side. Working into the wind will encourage this considerably.

To really groove or habituate this action the handler's use of voice and whistle will be necessary. The small size Acme or Roy Gonia whistle in plastic (not metal) is a necessary tool. The dog should be given two sharp toots on the whistle when he reaches the desired depth of thirty to forty yards in his casts to each side. Constant repetition for a half-dozen or more training sessions in the field will get the point over especially if first reinforced with a firm voice command. The wise handler will also accompany the turn signal with a wave of the hand indicating the direction of the next hunting cast, thus teaching both whistle and hand signals at the same time.

Voice commands should be held to a minimum and reserved for

Teaching a Springer to Quarter

Janet (Mrs. C. A.) Christensen, D.V.M., highly successful amateur trainer and handler, demonstrates the correct procedure for teaching a Springer to quarter. The dog is Greenbriar Gamekeeper.

The trainer here gets the dog's attention with whistle and hand signals. The dog is in the hupped position at this time.

The dog is sent to the trainer's left with a positive arm signal and the command HI ON.

The dog has completed his cast to the left, responded to the whistle command to reverse direction and receives a signal to cover the right side of his beat.

The dog now proceeds to quarter toward his right in response to the trainer's command.

great emergencies, and the dog encouraged to respond to the whistle and hand signals alone. It may be necessary for the handler at first to HUP the dog and dash out and scold him a bit if response to whistle is ignored in whole or in part.

Persistent effort and repetition will achieve the desired results. the young spaniel will never forget if properly taught and always enforced by the handler under all circumstances. It's wise also to occasionally HUP the working dog but don't nag him with the command every minute or two. A half-dozen HUPS in a thirty-minute workout when not in contact with game is desirable. Require the dog to sit for thirty seconds before ordering HI ON by voice command in the direction indicated by hand signal. This is a beneficial reinforcer. For exceptionally stubborn individuals a quick shot in the rump with a slingshot or BB gun (with spring reduced in strength) will improve response to whistle if used only occasionally. The electric collar is *not* recommended.

Correct Crosswind Pattern

A finished dog must learn to quarter properly on crosswind (wind blowing from one side) or downwind (wind blowing from rear on hunter's neck). In a crosswind a dog's natural inclination is to make a deep cast on the downwind side of handler and a short three-to five-yard cast on the upwind side of handler. His deep downwind casts can be controlled to normal thirty to forty yards by whistle commands (two sharp blasts on whistle to turn him). Trainer should always insist that dog make a complete 90 degree turn and not wander on down the course. As he swings back in response to whistle, at first give him constant hand signal direction to go to upwind side of handler. He won't at first but he will if he finds planted game 25 yards upwind from the path the handler will take. (Game can also be rolled in behind the dog when he is on his downwind beat. To roll in a bird, dizzy it with the head made to whirl exceedingly fast 10 to 20 times, then pitch the bird hard into a spot of cover upwind from the handler. Never, repeat never, let the dog see the bird being planted. When the dog returns from the downwind cast and is even with the handler, repeated hand directions and urging will eventually get him within scenting distance of the bird (thrown or pre-planted). A dozen or two such lessons and he'll whip upwind quickly when given the signal. It may be necessary to HUP the dog and send him back upwind a few times.

But it's a surefire method of widening his upwind casts, if he is handled into birds a few times. After he learns to respond to the hand signal reinforcer each time he is taken afield, he will learn to cast as deep upwind as he does downwind.

Downwind Pattern Routine

A spaniel's inclination on a downwind course is to slant down from the handler and loop back to him. This should be expanded to resemble a figure-8 pattern with half of the 8 to each side in front of the handler. This is an acceptable pattern since a dog cannot normally scent a bird downwind from him. The handler teaches the dog to hunt a downwind pattern by modifying the depth of downwind casts through whistle and hand signal control until the dog learns to perform figure-8 patterns in front of the handler. In this manner the dog covers ground to both sides downwind from the handler. If the dog is casting too wide and boring out too deep, he will respond better to commands and directions if he is called back into the few birds rolled in behind him. After a dozen call backs he'll spin on the whistle instantly and rush back to see what he missed. Once he responds to whistle and hand signals, it is only a matter of working him enough to let him learn the range he is to maintain at all times to find game and keep out of trouble. Usually he'll hunt wider and deeper in low cover than he will in high cover.

Introduction to Water

Retrieving from water is one of the chief functions of the complete spaniel gun dog, both for waterfowl shooting and upland game which may be dropped into a nearby stream or lake. Spaniels take to water with great enthusiasm with proper, early introduction. The proper time for the three- or four-months-old puppy is a warm sunny day in a small, warm water lake or pond with sloping banks. Begin by wading out from the bank a few yards to calf-deep water and ignoring the dog as he investigates all the strange new scents along the bank. Perhaps the youngster will follow his handler, but if not, he will venture in the water if called. After he wades in the shallows for a few minutes the handler should go out a little farther and urge the dog to follow to a depth which requires the youngster to swim a few splashing strokes. This may be enough for the first lesson. If the dog is enthusiastic about it, the handler may toss out

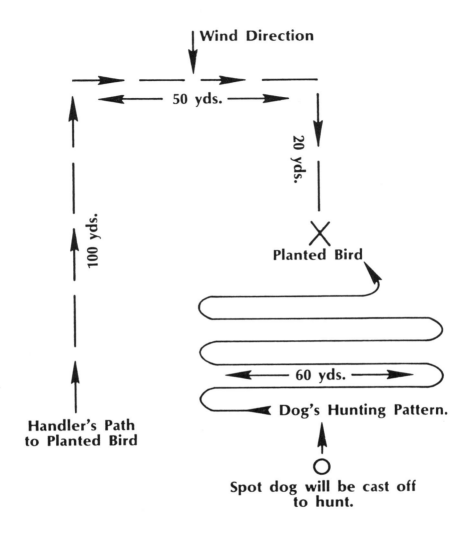

Wind Direction

50 yds.

20 yds.

100 yds.

X
Planted Bird

60 yds.

Dog's Hunting Pattern.

Handler's Path
to Planted Bird

O
Spot dog will be cast off
to hunt.

This diagram illustrates a method of bird planting to prevent a dog from trailing the handler's scent to the planted bird. It also illustrates the correct hunting pattern for a dog working into the wind.

110

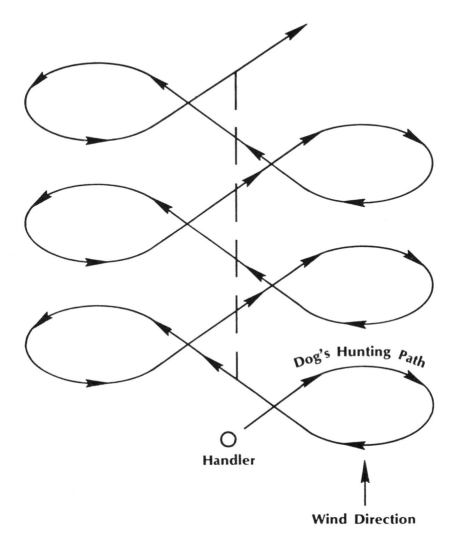

Dog's Hunting Path

Handler

Wind Direction

This diagram illustrates a normal, downwind hunting pattern for a flushing dog. A flushing dog's natural inclination to punch out downwind then swing back upwind to the handler can be modified and controlled. This is done by casting him to the side and turning him with the whistle so that his downcourse distance becomes a modified figure-eight hunting pattern always within normal gun range.

the canvas buck ten feet and urge the puppy to fetch it. Because he has learned to retrieve on land he may half swim and splash out to fetch the buck to hand. If not, a few more trips to the pond will build up his confidence in swimming out for a few yards to collect the buck and return it.

Most young dogs will drop the buck once they reach shore to shake themselves. To avoid this undesirable conduct the handler should walk backwards from water as he urges the spaniel to hold the buck and deliver to hand. Obviously much petting and praise should be the reward for completing the retrieve as for all other desirable responses to command.

After the first two or three sessions of being steady at the water, and when it is apparent that the pupil enjoys the work, he should be required to remain HUPPED at heel for a few seconds after the buck is thrown and the pistol fired before being sent to fetch on command. Steadying him to flush and shot at the water should be no problem when he reaches the six months stage since he has already learned it for land retrieving in his earlier yard work.

Double Water Retrieves

The next step at six or seven months of age is to toss two bucks after the pistol is fired at medium distance (twenty yards) before sending the dog to fetch. He'll usually collect the last one thrown, and then may be reluctant to go for the other. Give direction by extending forearm in front of the dog's eyes with voice commands of Spot FETCH. If the handler makes a vigorous throwing motion in the direction of the buck, it speeds up learning. With a slow learner, a rock tossed near the buck a few times will get him on the way to the second retrieve when he sees the splash. He will soon learn to go out for the second and even the third one, but always have something for the dog to retrieve—never fool him! The length of retrieves may gradually be extended to 40 or 50 and 75 yards finally, for both singles and doubles as he matures and learns to enjoy water retrieving.

Blind and Cold Blind Retrieves

The finished water retriever must also learn to make blind retrieves (dog did not see the buck thrown) from the water and to work through decoys. Have a friend station himself on a point on the opposite bank and toss the buck or a dead pigeon (which the dog did

The English Springer Spaniel, Saighton's Sleet, sight locked intensely on the path of the bird.

Talbot Radcliffe with his British National Champion Saighton's Sentry. Radcliffe is one of Britain's leading exponents of the field-bred Springer. He has imported many of his Saighton dogs to the United States where they have performed with great competence. Radcliffe's book *Spaniels for Sport* is recognized as one of the most definitive books available on training flushing dogs.

113

The English Springer Spaniel, Double National Amateur Field Ch. Sunray of Chrishall, executes a sensational water entry in his eagerness to retrieve a shot bird for his owner-handler Dr. Warren Wunderlich. Ray's consistent and impressive win record includes back-to-back National Amateur Championships, runner-up in the National Open Championship and a host of other fine wins.

Texas trainer David Jones knows trained gun dogs need some fun and relaxation occasionally. Here (far dog) Double Champion Strong's Seamus, Saighton's Sleet and Strong's Swanson are permitted to race for a thrown bird, knowing this is play time.

not see) AFTER he fires the blank pistol. The shot will arouse the spaniel's interest and cause him to head out into the water on command when given the direction.

He may attempt to return without the bird or buck the first time or two, but again a tossed rock, hand signals and the command BACK Spot will be helpful. Once he learns there is always something to retrieve when he is ordered into the water, he'll head out and search for it with his eyes and eventually with his nose. When he reaches this stage of development the gun can be eliminated. He will then learn to head out and search for cold, blind retrieves (did not see the object or the bird fall and did not hear a gun) when given the direction. This is a highly useful attribute in a hunter's duck dog which may be sent to collect shot game only after considerable time has elapsed.

Working through Decoys

Teaching a dog to work around decoys without becoming tangled or trying to fetch them is relatively simple. Begin the lessons by placing a decoy on shore near the water in early water work. After the youngster has checked it out a few times with his eyes and nose he should be given a firm NO Spot as he approaches it. After he learns to ignore the wooden or plastic decoy on shore, it may be anchored in the water five yards from shore during retrieving sessions and Spot ordered firmly to ignore it. Additional decoys may be added and anchored farther out in deeper water. Eventually, in spite of commands, the young dog will become tangled in decoy anchor lines. After several such occurrences, and with some urging and direction from handler, he will learn to take direction and swim around the edges to avoid the decoys.

Introduction to Duck

The use of live, clipped-wing pigeons should be substituted for the canvas buck for a few sessions of the water work. Then live pigeons, which are thrown from the shore and shot over the water by a friend, should be added to the training routine.

If the trainer expects to use the dog on duck and other waterfowl, his water work should be finished off with domestic mallard ducks. A few water retrieves with a dead duck will help him adjust to the larger-size bird and so will a half-dozen or more shot for him in the next two or three training sessions. It's well at this stage, or even an earlier one, to teach the dog to HUP quietly in a small brush blind and remain sitting for five minutes after several bucks, pigeons or dead ducks have been tossed in the water and a gun discharged.

If early obedience work in the yard and field has been thoroughly taught, even though highly excited by the shots and eager to go, a spaniel can be controlled by command and forced to sit in the blind until ordered to retrieve. Directing him to the objects or birds to be retrieved will test the degree of finish. If weaknesses show up in any areas, the trainer should return to the earlier training routines for a refresher course in obedience, response to hand signals or retrieving manners.

Finishing the Dog in the Field: Trailing Moving Game

The spaniel is now 12 to 15 months old, hunts with enthusiasm, quarters his ground well, is steady to flush and shot, responds to whistle, voice and hand signals, and completes marked and blind retrieves from land and water. His education is complete except for the important factors of learning to handle moving game and where to search for native game. The ability to perform both functions is essential if he is to qualify as a finished gun dog.

One way to start is with clipped-wing pigeons which are planted in six or eight inch cover without the dog observing it. Usually after a ten minute delay the birds will walk fifty yards or more leaving a line of scent in the cover. When the dog strikes the foot scent of a bird he may lower his head and follow the scent immediately, especially if the bird has been dampened with water and put down on a good scenting day. Perhaps he will make a false start or two or overrun the scent in his excitement. Eventually he will learn to trail the bird quickly and catch and retrieve it to hand. Spring, with scenting conditions good from the moisture in the ground, is the best time to work the young prospect on moving game. But it can be done in other seasons of the year. The guinea fowl, often difficult to obtain, is superior for this work as it moves farther and faster when its flight feathers are pulled from one wing. This bird speeds up the youngster's learning and provides a severe test of control when it is flushed and flies a few yards with much flapping and squawking. It also conditions Spot to carry a larger bird. The Chukar partridge, with flight feathers removed from one wing, may also produce the same results.

The English Springer Spaniel, Cripple Creek LeRoi, delivers a shot Mourning Dove to the author.

Dr. David McCurdy's great Springer Canadian Field Champion Saighton's Sort with mixed-bag game which he found, flushed and retrieved. The birds are pheasant, grouse and Jack Snipe.

117

The next step in the training routine calls for hen pheasants to be planted for the dog. The first few should be sailed out with the flight feathers removed from one wing. The dog will show much more animation on pheasants than on pigeons which gives the trainer an opportunity to sharpen him up on the stop whistle. Pheasants duck their heads and run on occasion, and the finished pheasant dog must respond instantly to the voice or whistle command to HUP when trailing moving game. Stopping the young dog several times at reasonable gun range, and insisting that he remain at the HUP position until the handler walks up and gives the orders to resume trailing, is the proper training sequence. Eventually he should be permitted to catch the clipped-wing pheasant and retrieve it to hand.

When the youngster learns with good manners, to trail game positively and is rewarded by catching and retrieving the non-flyer, it's time to work him on pheasants which will be flushed, shot and retrieved. Hen pheasants should be used for this phase. A crippled cock will struggle more which may encourage a smart spaniel to become hard-mouthed when he clamps down hard to hold the bird. A dozen or more game farm pheasants which are shot for the dog, with a few pigeons interspersed, give excellent experience and teach the trainer much about the dog's ability and temperament. If the hard buck has been used almost daily for a half dozen retrieves in the yard or field, Spot is less likely to clamp down on the game he retrieves.

Work on Native Game

The eager spaniel is now ready for work on native (wild) birds found in weed fields near a city or on nearby farms which have cover and feed during closed hunting season. But the trainer must follow an important training technique when working dogs on game which is not to be shot. The objective is to prevent the dog from pottering on stale scent left by last night's rabbits or game birds which moved through the cover. At this stage of the schooling, the handler should have learned when the dog strikes hot scent by his animation and tail action. Pottering occurs when the dog lowers his head and nose close to the ground and makes little or no forward progress. It is a fault due to inexperience. When he potters he should be cast off the scent and required to resume quartering on down the field. If the scent freshens the dog will telegraph it by his eagerness and may then be

118

permitted to work it out. A hen with a brood of chicks will leave much scent and so will a brace of half grown rabbits lurking in a briar patch or fence row. Requiring the dog to be steady to flush and shot—a blank pistol may be fired during non-hunting seasons—is good training. It speeds the dog on the way to learn WHERE and HOW to hunt and handle wild pheasant which he must learn on his own from frequent exposure to cover and game in repeated trips to the field. During this exposure to native game, which moves faster and uses many tricks to outwit both dog and man, experienced handlers take the opportunity to cast the dog off the line if the scent is not strong and require him to resume quartering. Not always easy, it is a highly useful accomplishment when hunting. The dog learns this response if the trainer is persistent and firm. Again, repetition creates the desired response as indicated by the psychological rule: "Success reinforces and produces similar behavior."

Hunting Spaniel on Native Game

Your fine young spaniel is hunting well and with much enthusiasm, is disciplined and under control. *Now* all you need—to make him a finished and complete gun dog—is to expose him to the real thing. This, of course, is more and more hunting. If you will insist that he follow the routines he learned by working within gun range, remaining steady to flush and shot, and turning on the whistle at proper range, you are on your way to having a top flushing dog.

Remember to give him occasional refresher courses during the off season. Then he will remain the fine, well-mannered gun dog into which you poured so much effort to achieve his high and most satisfactory education. We hope you have a dandy.

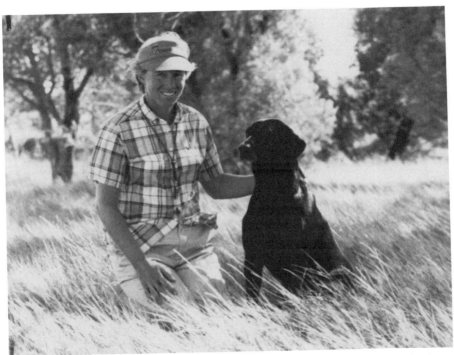

1984 National Amateur Field Champion Trumarc's Zip Code, a bold black Labrador Retriever, owned, handled and trained from puppyhood by Judy Aycock of Texas. She is the only woman to handle a retriever to the National Open Championship which she did in the 1976 NFC at San Joaquin Honcho. Her lifetime record includes having trained and handled 12 retrievers which became both Amateur and Open Field Champions and two others which earned Amateur Champion titles, a remarkable list of achievements.

7

How to Train Retrievers

A WELL-TRAINED NON-SLIP retriever should heel the hunter through cover, or sit quietly in a blind or duck boat, and retrieve any upland game and waterfowl shot, with a soft and tender mouth and only on command. He must willingly accept direction to blind retrieves and be a well-mannered, quiet, willing aid to the gun. The process of converting a six- or eight-week-old retriever to an eighteen-months-old finished dog requires a number of disciplined, controlled training routines and simulated hunting experiences before one can reach the desired goals.

The suggested training routines are described in detail in the following pages. The time sequence for introducing the several training routines is given below in outline form. But some variance in the time sequence may be required by three factors: the motivation and effort of the trainer, the temperament and learning speed of the dog, and the climatic conditions. Actually, the experienced trainer knows how to combine and teach two or more disciplines and routines and thus achieve desired results in a much shorter time span. The first-time trainer should follow the general outline and not introduce a new routine until Junior is proficient in the ones preceding it.

Early Yard Work—Eight to Twelve Weeks of Age

1. Socialize the puppy with several daily play periods and short walks on land. Teach him his name.

2. Begin early retrieving with knotted hand towel and hand clap.
3. Switch to small canvas boat bumper dummy during retrieving sessions after one week.
4. Begin early lessons in SIT, COME and STAY in response to voice commands.
5. Introduce cap pistol to daily five-minute retrieving sessions and at feeding time.
6. If the water and air temperatures are at least 55 degrees, introduce the puppy to water retrieving.
7. Teach the puppy to get in motion, to enter an enclosure and to respond to the command NO.

Three to Six Months of Age

1. Continue daily yard work and retrieving, but require more exacting performance gradually.
2. Substitute large canvas boat bumper buck and switch from the cap pistol to the blank pistol.
3. Introduce to the hard buck with feathers.
4. Introduce whistle commands to SIT and COME.
5. STEADY dog to sthrown buck in the yard retrieving.
6. Introduce to simple double yard retrieves.
7. Introduce to simple double land retrieves in field.
8. Begin with dead pigeons, then thrown live shackled pigeons, first on land, then in water retrieving—dog to be steady to bird and pistol shot.
9. Introduce to live, shot pigeons for single land and then water retrieving.

Six to Nine Months of Age

1. Continue yard retrieving and yard discipline at least twice weekly—in twenty-minute sessions.
2. Expand retrieving on land and water to doubles with shot pigeons and increasing distance gradually from 25 to 100 yards and spread expanded from 25 to 100 yards.
3. Ground dog thoroughly on all voice and whistle commands.
4. Work in hand directions on the second bird of double retrieve.

Nine to Twelve Months of Age

1. Continue yard work disciplines and retrieving twice weekly and expect perfect response at all times.

2. Continue to shoot doubles for the dog on land and water, but eliminate direction on fall of the second bird to test and improve marking memory.
3. Introduce to pheasants in land retrieving sessions with a few thrown dead birds, then with live, shot birds.
4. Begin early blind retrieving on land with simple short falls. Work in hand signals.
5. Increase distance of blind retrieves and work in some doubles.

Twelve to Eighteen Months of Age

1. Continue yard work and yard retrieving at least twice a week.
2. Shoot domestic mallards over water for marked retrieve.
3. Continue, with on-land and in-water cold (no shot), blind retrieves with pigeons and game.
4. Work decoys into water retrieving.
5. Plan to plug up any holes that appear in the dog's performance by more effort and work.
6. Take the dog hunting for any wild game, ranging from doves to geese, at every opportunity. If the season is not open, work him on released birds at a Put and Take game farm. Work and use him as much as possible. If the dog performs well, the game farm owner may invite you to work him for a customer for free! It's great experience!
7. Enter the dog in a spring or fall puppy stake at a retriever field trial. Compare his work with other puppy entries as a measure of his progress and the degree of finish.

Training a Retriever Puppy Gun Dog

The first and most important step in training a retriever to become a good gun dog is to find a prospect bred from dogs which have been hunted for several generations. For two reasons *buy* a dog and do not accept one as a gift from some friend or neighbor. You will have a better and selective choice in the breeding, age, color and other desirable factors. And investing one's own cash usually increases the owner's interest and appreciation for the dog and motivates him to further its education through the necessary training effort.

The dog should be from hunting stock, because individuals from bloodlines which have not been hunted for four or five generations have missed the "culling" used by hunting dog breeders

1986 Canadian National Champion Big River Bonne Annie, Labrador female with handler Mike Bardy. Annie, owned by Mrs. John Romadka of Wisconsin, was Open and Amateur Champion in 1984. In 1985 she took time to whelp a litter and in 1986 won the national title.

Maxim Cash Chester, a show Champion Chesapeake Bay Retriever, which owner Kevin Marks of Kansas has trained to hunt. Dual type gun dogs of any breed are somewhat rare.

who quickly dispose of stock which does not produce acceptable gun dogs. Though all dogs will hunt, *how* they hunt is the key factor. Through selective breeding and testing of each generation in the field, this man-made contribution to nature's survival of the fittest emphasizes the desirable characteristics. Good gun dogs do not just happen in any breed. They represent the effort of thousands of dedicated dog owners who have worked for hundreds of years to produce better hunting dogs. So the wise hunter takes advantage of this fact by buying a puppy from hunting dog stock with several generations of hunting ancestors behind it.

What to Look for in the Pedigree

How can a prospective owner determine that a specific litter of retriever puppies comes from hunting stock and not from pet or show bloodlines? One measure is to check four or five generation pedigrees of a puppy for field champions—several with a prefix F.Ch, A.F.C., N.F.C. or N.A.F.C. which translates into Field Champion, Amateur Field Champion, National Field Champion, or National Amateur Field Champion. One or two such prefixes in each generation is proof positive of hunting stock behind the puppy. Another way to determine field, show or pet bloodlines is to consult a reputable breeder of hunting stock. Such a person can give you guidance. Many will be found in the *Retriever Field Trial News*. A further source of information is a local professional gun dog trainer known to the local sporting goods store owner or to the local gun club. They will probably know the location and date of the closest retriever field trial where the prospective buyer can find many people who can tell him where to buy field bred stock, and may also offer other useful suggestions.

What are field trials? They are simulated, competitive hunting exercises for trained retriever gun dogs, which are tested for their retrieving skills and ability to accept training kindly. This fast growing sport—there were 211 retriever, 47 spaniel, and 420 pointing trials in America in 1986—has done more to improve the retriever breeds than any other single factor. Field trials also provide much challenging recreation for thousands of hunters in schooling an animal to perform to the top level of his native ability. Amateur trainer-owners are becoming increasingly more successful and more active. These dedicated men and women have improved the hunting desire and trainability of the present day retrievers.

Retrievers are first, last and always the best dogs in the world for fetching shot game. The training routines in this section will emphasize a method of developing a non-slip retrieving dog rather than a flushing dog which hunts before the gun. A non-slip retrieving dog walks at the hunter's heel, or sits in a duck blind, a boat or a dove field, and retrieves to his owner all the game shot from land or water. Retriever owners who expect to use their dogs for finding and flushing game before the gun should read the sections on quartering, Starting Young Dogs on Live Game, Steady to Flush and Shot and related topics in Chapter 6.

The puppy's education may begin when he is eight weeks old by his simultaneous introduction to early retrieving and simple yard work where he learns to respond to the basic commands. Both the suggested routines for retrieving and yard work may be included in daily training sessions. He will learn to love them.

Apropos of the acquisition of a field bred retriever and the importance of field trials in the enjoyment of a dog are the comments of Mr. Charles L. Hill of Bellevue, Washington.

Mr. Hill, together with his wife, owns the great Labrador Ch. Wanapum Dart's Dandy, winner of the National Open Championship in 1975 and the National Amateur Championship in 1976. Handled by his owner, this super field dog outperformed an entry of 68 in eleven series. One of these was a 200-yard cold blind. Highly skilled amateurs and professionals alike competed here and it was Dandy that carried the day to bring him the Open title. He met and bested a field of 83 in ten series to take the National Amateur crown.

Here are Charles Hill's useful observations on the education of a retriever gun dog:

Field trial retrievers are superior hunters and should be hunted on all types of game. Field trialing is an enjoyabe off-season sport, which keeps the dog tuned and helps you evaluate your training progress.

Choose a retriever pup out of the best possible breeding, raise it in the house and let the children participate in the training. Be firm, but kind, and never ask the dog to start anything you do not expect it to complete. Be consistent. While training your dog, in the field or in your home, concentrate on teaching and showing your dog what you expect. Never take the style and the joy out of your retriever by overwork or too much stress. Have fun with your dog and the reward will be enjoyed through many years of companionship and mutual cooperation.

Response to Basic Commands

Instant response to the six basic commands are the foundations for all gun dog schooling and all must be learned by the dog until they become a reflex response. The command COME coupled with the puppy's name can be taught and quickly learned during feeding time, that is JUNIOR COME, and with food the motivator and with gratification of hunger the reinforcer.

During the socializing routines all puppies need and must have, as covered in Chapter 6, Junior can get further schooling on COME and learning his name by being called and presented with a tidbit and much petting.

If Junior has a bold and independent spirit, a light cord may be attached to his collar and he can be gently brought to heel with tidbit, voice and hand rewards. This training routine should be started the second or third day after Junior arrives in his new home. Use of the light string checkcord will also teach Junior to lead. If it is not used, as described above, a few trips around the yard with a leather lead attached to his collar, and some coaxing and frequent stops for petting, will soon teach him to lead and perhaps shorten the period of his desire to imitate the actions of a Brahman bull calf at a rodeo roping contest.

Teaching Puppy to SIT

When the COME, name and lead response have been mastered, begin schooling the youngster to sit. Start the action by leading the youngster around the secluded training area on the short lead. No children, other dogs or other distractions should be present. Junior should be at the trainer's left heel if the trainer is right-handed, or at the right heel for left-handed people. The trainer comes to a stop and presses down on Junior's hips while giving the command SIT. Hand pressure should be applied for four or five seconds to keep him sitting the first few times. After five seconds handler should command HEEL and resume walking while keeping the lead tight enough to force the puppy to walk close to his leg. The first lesson should be restricted to five minutes as the puppy is given the command SIT eight or ten times. Future lessons may be increased gradually for longer periods. The puppy should learn the command and response in the first lesson so that pressure on his hips is no longer necessary.

Dual Ch. Tiger's Cub, CD, Chesapeake Bay Retriever, owned by Eloise H. Cherry. At age eleven, he was still siring winners in bench and field. Mrs. Cherry was one of America's prime exponents of the dual purpose Chesapeake.

Arkansas duck hunters Ron Branaman and Steve Monte, Jr. with Labrador Retriever Babe, sit in a portable 5 lb. duck blind and wait for early season Teal.   *Goodall*

Teaching Puppy to STAY

Some trainers combine the response for sit and stay into the one command SIT. Learning to respond to the command STAY, however, is useful to prevent a dog from bolting from the automobile, rushing from the residence or kennel door and in other situations. One can usually teach this to the puppy by commanding SIT—SIT—SIT, or STAY—STAY—STAY depending on the decision to teach one or both commands. Petting and voice rewards are given for correct response. If Junior is a slow learner on STAY, attach both ends of a light checkcord to his collar after passing it around a small tree, stake in the ground or water pipe in the basement or the garage. Then force him to stay by pulling on one end of the checkcord. The trainer can also speed up the response to the command COME at the same time by pulling the other end of the checkcord and forcing the dog to come to heel. This technique is used only to teach the dog what is required when other training fails to penetrate. Its use should be limited to one or two lessons at the most. Requiring the dog to sit, stay and come with the checkcord dragging will serve as a reminder that he must respond properly.

The youngster should enjoy the training sessions. He will if they are kept short and he is suitably rewarded each time, Puppies have a short span of attention and a ten or twelve-weeks-old puppy cannot be expected to sit and stay very long. Two or three minutes is not too much to expect of the three-months-old dog. If he "breaks" (refuses to stay) severe punishment is not called for. Instead he should be picked up, carried back to the spot and commanded to STAY in a firm voice coupled with a shake or two. Common sense and careful observation of the dog's response should guide the trainer's actions at all times. Losing one's temper is the cue for the trainer to stop the session and return the puppy to his kennel for at least 24 hours. Puppies have long memories for trauma-producing punishment. The wise trainer will be moderate in punishment, and in rewards too, after the dog has learned the desired behavior response. The overreward is given only when the puppy is very young.

Teaching Puppy to Get in Motion

Teaching the youngster to respond to the command HI-ON, meaning to get in motion, can be done quickly by using the command HI-ON each time the puppy is released in the field or yard

A check cord and wooden stake are handy aids in retriever training. With the check cord passed around the stake and both ends fixed to the dog's collar, the trainer gives the SIT command and forces the dog into position as shown. *Goodall*

To teach the command COME, the trainer gives the command and pulls the right side of the cord at the same time.

Goodall

To teach the dog STAY, the trainer gets the dog to SIT and STAY when the dog is half-way to him. A gentle tug on the cord enforces the command. *Goodall*

to chase grasshoppers or to check out last night's slightly stale rabbit scent. If the command HI-ON is accompanied by pointing arm to right or left with the trainer taking a step or two in the same direction, the ground work for learning hand signals will be laid. Since it's good canine psychology to end each training session by permitting the dog a few minutes to do pretty much as he likes, he will quickly learn that HI-ON command means it's recess or coffeebreak time. It strengthens handler's control to release him with this command than merely to unsnap the lead and let Spot wander away without command or direction.

Teaching Puppy to Enter an Enclosure

A hunting dog must respond to owner's command to enter an automobile, a kennel, the dog crate in a station wagon or pick-up or any other enclosure. The commands KENNEL UP or LOAD UP are most frequently used. The youngster will soon learn what the command means if it is given to him each time he is put into his kennel, the car or other enclosure. Learning what the owner wants him to do must often be punctuated with a push or slight pressure with the lead to get the necessary compliance. The same command should be used every time with insistence that the puppy obey. A young dog may be carsick the first few times he travels by automobile. Encouraging him to climb in the vehicle or carry-crate in several ten minute sessions, with plenty of vocal and petting rewards, will teach him he must comply and may help to overcome carsickness. This may be the result of fear of the car as well as motion sickness. But when he associates the car with a trip afield he'll be cured overnight. A six-months-old dog should hop into the car or his carry-crate just as fast (instantly) when the hunting or training session is ended as he does at home when he knows he is going hunting.

How to Teach Puppy the Response to Command NO

The command NO, with or without the dog's name preceding it, is the owner's most useful tool to cause Junior to stop instantly whatever he is doing. If this is a house dog he will learn its meaning quickly if he starts to chew on a rug or one of mama's new shoes. The command NO, accompanied if needed by a light swat over the rear with a folded newspaper or a flyswatter, will speed up the learning process. It can also be taught by insisting at mealtimes that he not eat for a minute or two until given the O.K. To begin, place the feed pan on the ground or floor and restrain the puppy physically while repeating NO—NO—NO. Beginning with a ten-second delay the first few times, gradually increase to a few minutes before releasing him verbally. A three-months-old puppy should learn to refrain from eating at command NO for several seconds without physical restraint by lead or by the trainer's hands. Once he has progressed this far he can be stopped from rolling in fresh cow manure, working a snake, or chewing up the upholstery in the automobile. In other words he will have learned that NO means stop what you are doing *now*.

Early Preparation for the Gun

Gun-shyness is a man made affliction in most cases. It will never occur if the trainer takes a little time to introduce the youngster to the gun. A cap pistol fired at feeding time fifteen yards away from the puppy is an ideal way to begin. A week later it can be fired several times at five yards' distance from the feeding puppy and he will ignore it. If he does flinch, move back some distance and gradually move in closer to the dog during the next week. The cap pistol should also be used in connection with the puppy's early retrieving.

Early Retrieving Routine for the Puppy

In most cases it's not necessary to teach a retriever puppy to pick up and carry an object. The instinct to do so is often so strong that the youngster will begin carrying sticks or small rocks or his feed pan around at a very early age. It *is* necessary to channel this instinct, developed through several hundred years of careful breeding and selection, into dependable disciplined response. The necessary tools for the first phase include a small size canvas boat bumper approximately four to five inches in circumference, a large one approximately ten to twelve inches in circumference. It must be canvas and NOT plastic. The third object is a hard retrieving buck of wood with a metal sleeve; see the description of this in the spaniel section.

Since retrieving is the single most important contribution the puppy will make to his owner's sport of hunting, the prospect should learn it correctly from the beginning. And the time to begin is when

A retriever must be trained to enter an automobile, crate or other enclosure on command. To commence this training with Lucky, she has been given the FETCH command to bring in a retrieving buck which has been tossed into the back of a pickup truck. This early training will later result in a most easily manageable dog on hunting trips.   *Goodall*

he is eight-weeks-old. A small knotted towel or handkerchief makes a good starting object. If Junior is teased with it enough to arouse his interest before it is tossed three or four feet away, he will probably seize it in his mouth and head off in the opposite direction. This is the time to call, clap hands and back away from him. This should encourage him to come to the trainer with the object. A secluded area with no distractions is essential, and some cajoling will probably cause him to bring it to hand the first time. When he does, the handler should give much vocal and physical reward and gently remove the object from the puppy's mouth while softly repeating GIVE. A blind, narrow hallway or a kennel run will contribute to the youngster's coming to heel with the bundle.

A half dozen retrieves will be enough for the first five minute lesson, and petting and praise will help Junior enjoy the action. If he refuses to pick it up, more teasing and continued effort will eventually secure the desired result. If he is reluctant to return with the object, a long, light string attached to his collar and pulled gently by the handler will serve to guide his return. A dozen two-a-day sessions will teach Junior that he is rewarded only when he brings the object to hand. He should be performing well within a day or two. Later, two blasts on the whistle can be added to the routine to signal the dog to return.

If he is reluctant to give up the object on the soft command GIVE, blowing in his nose will usually produce the desired result. After twenty or thirty successful retrieves with the cloth object, switch to the small canvas buck described earlier. He will probably pick it up the first time if teased with it for a few seconds. Any deviation from the desired response with the canvas buck can be corrected with the actions described above—the light checkcord, blowing in his nose (or ear) or the handler moving away from the puppy.

If these sessions are continued daily just after his short schooling sessions on COME, STAY, etc., he should progress to the point of eagerly anticipating the sessions and performing the exercises nearly perfectly each time. The handler should have accompanied each toss of the canvas buck with a sharp handclap, or discharge of the cap pistol, to simulate the noise of a gun.

It will be assumed that Junior is now twelve weeks old, performing well in his yard work and retrieving the small canvas buck with eagerness from land up to a distance of thirty or forty yards. He is ready to move on to the larger canvas buck which he should handle well after a half-dozen sessions. With this transition successfully accomplished and no recurring problems present, he is ready for his first exposure to feathers. An excellent device for this purpose is the hard buck described in the spaniel chapter of this book. The metal sleeve is to discourage Junior from biting or chewing as some youngsters at this age might attempt to do. And so may Junior. If he is well-grounded in the command COME, HEEL, or the come-in whistle given *after* he has the buck in his mouth, this should eliminate the problem of his taking off to bury it, or stopping to chew it. He may stop to check it thoroughly with his nose on his first first exposure to feathers—even long dead ones attached to the buck. If he refuses to pick it up on first exposure after a few stern commands of Junior FETCH, he will usually get the message if he is teased with it a few times and accepts it as another part of this pleasant game of retrieving for the boss. If he flatly refuses to pick up the feathered buck or any other object for any reason, his kind—one in a thousand—will often change their mind if restrained at heel near another dog making retrieves from land or water.

Steadying to Flush

Up to this point the emphasis has been on letting Junior chase the single thrown buck to make him enthusiastic about retrieving. The next step in his education is teaching him to retrieve *only* on command. When he is five or six months old his training should reach the stage where he is ready to learn to sit at heel and remain sitting until released by the command to make the retrieve (simulated ready to flush). Since he learned to sit and stay in early yard work, it's easy to steady him to the thrown buck.

Begin the first lesson by standing in front of the dog. Order him to SIT and STAY and toss the buck over your shoulder a few feet to the rear. If the puppy attempts to retrieve, grab him and physically but gently force him to sit. After a pat or two give the command FETCH and wave him in the direction of the buck. Several short lessons in this routine should get the point over that he must wait for the command. Next, move to the right side of the sitting dog and step on the lead or checkcord attached to the dog's collar before tossing the buck. Foot pressure on the lead will force the dog to remain sitting when reinforced with the commands to STAY, STAY, STAY. After a half-dozen five-minute lessons the foot pressure can

A buck has been thrown out for Lucky to retrieve, but after picking it up she decides not to take it to the trainer.

Goodall

Early yard work pays off. Responding to a whistle command, Lucky rights herself and heads directly for the trainer.

Goodall

"Thatta girl." Lucky delivers the buck nicely to hand.

Goodall

136

be eliminated, and after another equal number of lessons the lead or checkcord can be eliminated completely. As the lessons continue the length of the retrieves and the training period can be extended. It's good training discipline for the dog if the handler occasionally walks out and picks up the buck while insisting that the dog remain at SIT position. If the dog leaves before the command, the handler should make every effort to get to the buck before the dog does. Then he should pick up the puppy and carry him back to the spot he left while repeating a few stern words like BAD DOG and NO. A shake or two when the dog is placed on the ground serves as a reinforcer. Junior soon learns that he must wait for the command before he retrieves, and will have completed an important part of his basic education. But even though he has learned what he should do, it will require constant vigilance and an occasional swat with the lead to convince him that there can be no deviation.

Sit or Stand to Deliver Retrieved Object

At this point the handler should decide whether he wants his dog to sit before delivering a retrieved object or merely bring it to hand. Sitting to deliver a retrieved dummy or bird gives slightly more control of the dog fetching a crippled bird and is a visual demonstration of good manners. It is recommended. Junior learned to sit in his yard training for several different routines. A few minutes devoted to requiring him to sit immediately in front of the handler when he returns with the retrieved buck is the way to begin. After several dozen retrieves it will soon become automatic for the dog to anticipate the command. If he sits too far from the handler he will soon learn to deliver to hand if commanded to HEEL while hands are extended palm out at handler's sides. The handler must be consistent in this as in all other commands, if he expects the dog to be consistent. In other words, do it the same way each time. Select one command for each desired action and stick to it.

Double Retrieves

When young dogs are first exposed to the feathered buck, they often prefer it to the canvas buck. A trainer can accomplish two objectives if he uses both the feathered buck and the large canvas buck while teaching the dog to make double retrieves. Double retrieves are most important as they form the basic first steps for multiple and blind retrieving. This is important for the duck blind and all pass shooting where the dog may not be sent to retrieve until several birds are in the water or on the ground. He must learn to go back for a second, third or even more birds, and take hand signal directions too.

With the dog at the handler's left heel begin the double retrieve lessons by tossing the feathered and canvas bucks some ten yards away and about ten yards apart. Order the dog to retrieve, and expect him to go to the last buck thrown as most dogs will do. When he picks it up immediately give him a come in whistle. After he sits and delivers give him a quick direction with the left arm in front of his nose and the command to FETCH. He may rush out and retrieve the second buck too. But he may be slightly confused and move out a few yards, then stop and look at the handler. When this occurs, walk halfway to the buck while repeating BACK Junior, BACK. If necessary walk the first three or four times to within a few feet of the buck. Make sure the dog also finds the second buck. Then give him plenty of praise and petting. Try several more short doubles and hope he gets the message at this first session. If not, try again the next day until he does learn that there are two bucks to retrieve each time. (Birds thrown upwind from the dog will speed up the learning process.) Once he learns this, gradually increase the distance in succeeding lessons until he is making doubles at fifty yards distance with forty yards or so between the two bucks. It's important to prevent Junior from attempting to fetch both bucks at one time, which eventually he will try to do. Stop such undesirable action immediately with the come-in whistle when he has the first one in his mouth. Messing around trying to fetch two birds simultaneously or to switch birds can cause the loss of a cripple and is poor manners.

It is assumed that the handler has given a sharp clap of his hands each time he tosses a retrieving buck and has perhaps substituted a cap pistol for the hand clap in the single retrieves. Junior has learned that this noise is part of the act and will accept the substitution of the blank pistol while at heel when making double retrieves. Opinions vary, but it is suggested that the pistol be discharged for each bird thrown. This can be reduced to one shot later on when the dog is completing the second retrieve after learning and remembering to mark it. There should be no adverse reaction to the use of the pistol. If there is the handler can continue with the cap

Cotton Pershall, all-time great retriever trainer, with five National Open Championships to his credit says of training: "Patience is the main thing, repeating the stuff you have already shown the dog over and over again. There's no short cut."

Mr. and Mrs. Roy Gonia at a Springer trial where both were judging. Mr. Gonia is one of only two handlers to win a National Retriever and a National Springer trial. Their son, Jim, follows in his parents' footsteps as a successful professional.

pistol for another week and then return to the 22 blank. After three or four sessions with the 22, the trainer can substitute a 32 or 38 caliber blank pistol, or a shot gun loaded with poppers (shells containing no shot).

Introduction to Water

The climate and season of the year will have a bearing on the dog's first exposure to water retrieving. A puppy whelped in October could be put in the water in Florida or southern California in January, but not in Minnesota because he could not swim on ice. It is suggested that the puppy be taken to the water for the first time when the water and the air temperatures are 55 degrees or higher, and as soon as possible after he is eight or ten weeks old. If he is permitted to run free for ten minutes to check out all the lovely new scents, he may dash into the water. If really precocious, he might even swim a lick or two. The average puppy may need a little encouragement, and the boss can provide it by wading out a few feet and encouraging Junior to follow. Maybe he will and maybe he won't. A little effort will have him swimming puppy fashion with front feet splashing and head held high to avoid the splash. Tossing the small canvas buck a half-dozen times where he can reach it without swimming is good for openers. Then two or three slightly longer tosses requiring him to swim a lick or two is enough for the first session. But the session should be repeated again that day and several times each week until that first five-minute water routine has been extended to a session where he will complete ten or fifteen water retrieves at twenty yards distance. Then gradually increase to fifty yards and longer.

Junior has a deep instinct to shake the water from his coat immediately after he exits from the water, and this must be stopped before it becomes a habit. He must be trained to deliver the buck *before* he shakes. Standing at the water's edge to take the first half-dozen retrieves is one way to begin. The handler should move back gradually from the water on succeeding water retrieving sessions, insisting firmly each time by whistle and voice that Junior hurry to the handler with the buck before he does anything else. Why is this so important? If Junior, upon becoming an adult, lays down a crippled duck or goose to shake himself, he may have to spend twenty minutes recovering a crippled bird. This can also flare the next flight of waterfowl out of gun range. Also, it is poor, sloppy

140

work manners. The handler moving rapidly away from Junior, coupled with stern commands, can and will correct the stopping-to-shake habit. Require him to SIT to deliver, if that was the routine on land retrieves.

The remarks and suggestions outlined in this book are given to help the hunter who is training his first or second dog without help or assistance. An assistant to throw birds or bucks on land and water, and to discharge blank pistols, can be a great help. Even a non-hunting, non-shooting partner can be helpful in this regard, but we know of several cases where a previously non-doggy, non-hunting assistant became hooked and moved in on the action. This is good for the dog's education and the sport, as greater interest can lead to additional ways to improve the breed.

Retrieving Birds on Land

Introducing the young retriever to a bird can be accomplished with a cold, dead pigeon or a dead upland game bird. Begin by first giving him an opportunity to smell the dead bird for a minute or two. Make him sit at heel and toss the bird out to be retrieved. When he picks it up, whistle him in quickly, take the bird, and praise him. Repeat the process a dozen or more times, and if all goes well gradually increase the distance of the retrieve. If he is reluctant to pick it up the first few times, tease him a bit with the dead bird and try again until he does pick it up. Always insist that he return with it immediately and sit to deliver. Four or five ten-minute sessions with the cold, dead bird in the yard will be enough to arouse his interest and get him ready to retrieve shot birds.

It is a good idea to switch from the dead bird to a live, clipped-wing pigeon for a dozen retrieves to prepare him for those cripples he will have to fetch many times in his life. When he is performing well with the clipped-wing pigeons (clip the long flight feathers on one wing of the pigeon), it is time to shoot a few birds with a shot gun. For this routine a friend to do the shooting is a great help. The friend should be positioned some thirty yards in front of the dog and trainer and instructed to hold a bird in one hand and his gun in the other. He should call out sharply MARK until he gets the dog's attention. When this occurs he should sail out, with underhand throw, a live pigeon crosswind, and then shoot it cleanly. Junior should retrieve it on command. Because of early training he should perform well. After he has completed several dozen single retrieves

Steve Monte steps out of his portable blind to accept an early season Teal from his Labrador Suzy. *Chuck Goodall*

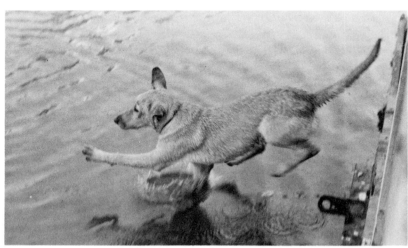

A Lab puppy is sent from a boat dock to retrieve in order to encourage a pattern of bold water entries. *Goodall*

of shot birds satisfactorily at fifty or more yards, he is ready for double retrieves. The assistant has probably missed and picked up one or two birds. That's O.K. because birds will be missed over the dog during open hunting season. This gives the trainer a chance to control the eager youngster and let him know he won't be sent to retrieve every time the gun is discharged. If unable to secure the services of a friend to shoot, the trainer will have to do the job himself. In such case, he should move five yards to one side and a step ahead of the sitting dog, and throw and shoot the birds himself. Veterans do this constantly, but the novice trainer is urged not to throw the gun and put the pigeon to his shoulder. It just won't work!

Double Retrieves of Shot Birds

Begin this procedure by placing the assistant thirty yards in front of the dog with instructions to sail out and shoot pigeons either downwind or crosswind. The assistant should try to have a forty-yard spread between the two shot birds. Junior is almost sure to go to the last bird shot for his first retrieve. Handler should call him in by whistle and take the bird. At the command HEEL the dog should swing around to the handler's left side (for right-handers), accept a quick signal from the handler's left arm bent at the elbow, pointing in the direction of the second bird, and commanded to FETCH.

Early training with bucks has taught him to mark fairly well, but he should learn to accept direction too. Ideally he should take a straight and fast line to the second bird, snatch it up and hurry back with it. If he is short of the fall, give the command BACK and make a throwing motion in the direction of the bird, but let him hunt it out a bit. He must learn to mark falls on the button and too much direction at this stage might make him too dependent. As Junior progresses with his marking, the falls can be increased to fifty to 75 and even 100 yards, occasionally in knee-high cover. The more experience he acquires marking and fetching longer and longer falls, the more accurate his marking becomes. But increases in distance and cover height should be gradual, never moving to more difficult terrain or retrieves until he is performing well on the simpler ones.

Double Retrieves from Water

If Junior has been introduced to shot doubles on land, there will be little or no problem about doubles shot for him over water. The

David Michael Duffey, noted dog editor of *Outdoor Life* and the author of several books, is pleased as the Springer Flirt excitedly delivers her first White-fronted Goose. As Duffey hoists the bird free, Dhu, the Labrador looks on with interest and perhaps a slight tinge of jealousy.

The late John Olin, an outstanding sportsman, enjoyed having a flushing dog at heel or riding in his wagon when hunting at his Nilo Plantation in Georgia. Olin snapped a photo of yellow Labrador Sunspot of Shamrock Acres finding a quail the bird dogs missed.

144

first few should be under forty yards. Place the shooter on a bank fifteen yards to one side or on a point of land on the opposite shore with the birds shot so they fall at a reasonable distance. If the dog becomes confused and reluctant to return for the second bird, he should catch on quickly if a few are shot closer and directly in front of him. The handler should insist at all times that the dog refrain from shaking, sit to deliver and demonstrate the good manners learned in early yard and retrieving sessions. No slackness should be permitted in any area of his work. Once the dog, now about nine months old, completes the double retrieves at forty or so yards, the distance and the spread between birds can be increased gradually to 75 yards. If the pigeon supply is not adequate, dead birds previously shot can be used, after gun or pistol shot. This technique allows for better control of distance and spread if they are tossed from the opposite shore or from an adjacent point of land.

Retrieving Ducks and Pheasant

At some stage in Junior's education as a complete land and water retriever he must be switched occasionally from inexpensive pigeons to larger, heavier pheasants and ducks. When he is eight or nine months old he should be started at first with dead and slightly stiff pheasants thrown out by hand for land retrieving. After he learns to carry cold, dead birds, the next step calls for a session or two on retrieving freshly killed pheasant. Some young dogs will pick up and drop and perhaps roll the bird around at first. If this occurs, the trainer is cautioned to speed up the action by urging the dog with whistle and voice commands. After a few attempts he'll succeed and be ready to have pheasant shot for retrieving.

An identical procedure is suggested for water retrieving with cold, dead ducks, then freshly killed ones followed by shot birds to acclimate him rapidly in the switch from pigeons to heavier birds. And Junior will like to switch because hand-raised, game farm birds have a much more gamey scent than do pigeons.

Breaking Flush or Shot

A dog's enthusiasm to retrieve increases substantially with the switch from the bucks to live, shot birds. Some place along the line he will certainly have a memory lapse and break flush or shot (attempt to retrieve without orders either when the bird is released or the gun discharged).

This calls for immediate corrective action. If possible the handler should outrun him to the bird, if the dog fails to stop at repeated whistle and verbal commands to SIT. If the dog arrives first and picks up the bird, it should be taken from him at once and the dog yanked back by his collar to the spot where he broke—and given a couple of sharp cuts with the lead, and some rough talk. The handler should force the dog to SIT while he walks out and picks up the bird. Perhaps this will suffice the first time he breaks. But if he does it again, the corrective treatment should be repeated and more force used to show him that he must stop on one whistle blast or voice command to SIT. With a hot, eager youngster a few sessions in the yard, in which dead and shackled live birds are thrown to within five yards of the dog by the assistant, may also be needed. If the trainer is at the dog's side with a long willow switch to freshen his memory, it will get results.

There are more severe forms of "attention getters," such as the cattle prod and the electric collar. They are not recommended for the novice trainer with his first dog. The trainer must go back to the yard and repeat early lessons of SIT, COME, STAY and others to drill Junior persistently and thoroughly with many thrown birds, coupled with pistol shot, on both land and water. This will eventually get results. But do not be discouraged. It's possible you have a very superior dog.

Blind Retrieves

Good gun dogs, especially retrievers and Springer Spaniels, must learn to complete blind retrieves (search for a bird they did not see fall). One way to begin this routine is to heel the dog downwind (wind blowing on handler's back) through cover. Next toss a buck or dead bird in the cover fifteen yards to trainer's right or left where the dog can see it, and continue walking for another 25 yards. Then SIT the dog and give him the command which he already knows—Junior FETCH. The odds are that he will race back and collect the object. The bird should be tossed some distance from the handler's path to keep the dog from learning to backtrail the handler's scent. After a few sessions with the distance gradually increased to fifty or sixty yards, plant a bird thirty yards upwind in low cover without the dog seeing it. Then from SIT position give him a direction signal with bent left arm and send him out with the command FETCH. If he marks short, which he may, make a throwing motion with right arm

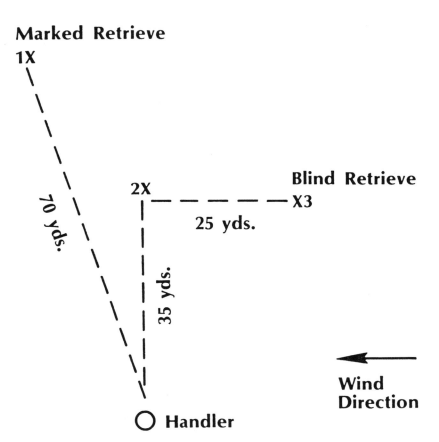

Marked Retrieve

1X

70 yds.

2X

Blind Retrieve

X3

25 yds.

35 yds.

Wind
Direction

O **Handler**

Starting a dog on blind retrieves; Begin by planting a bird at X3 which the dog is not permitted to see. Then give the dog a marked fall at X1. After completing the marked retrieve, send the dog to X2, ordering him to SIT. Give him a hand signal to the right together with the verbal command FETCH RIGHT. Much repetition will eventually bring the correct response to both verbal and hand signals. When the dog works reliably to the right, switch the blind fall to the left and teach the dog to work accordingly.

raised above the head and say Junior BACK. He may get the idea immediately but it may require much persistent repetition to teach him to hunt farther out. The handler may have to walk part way to the first few birds before the dog gets the idea. Once he has learned that the throwing motion and the command BACK mean hunt deeper, the length of the retrieves can gradually be increased until Junior goes out 100 or more yards to find the bird. The into-the-wind direction will help increase the distance because he can smell the bird better than a downwind or crosswind plant. His learned response to command to hunt farther away from the handler means that one-third of the work is done. Now he must learn to take directions to go right or left.

To Hunt Right or Left

Teaching retrievers to hunt to their right or left is slightly more difficult than to get them to go straight out. It helps to use both a verbal command and an arm direction signal to achieve this. Canine vision is excellent for motion. Observe how Junior can see a flying bird several hundred yards away from the car windows, but may lose the handler at forty yards in a field if one stands motionless.

So teach him the old teamster commands, GEE and HAW, or RIGHT and LEFT. Here is a way to start. Out of his sight plant a live, shackled pigeon twenty yards upwind to the right. Next sit dog and back away ten yards from him. As he turns automatically to face you, while he sits, make several waving motions with the right arm to the right and command FETCH RIGHT. It may take five or fifty sessions to get the correct response. Next use two falls—one a seventy yard marked and crosswind, and the other a 25 yard upwind blind fall about fifteen yards off the line of direction of the marked fall. After he completes the marked fall send him out again, but SIT him with the whistle downwind from the blind. Give him the proper hand signal and command FETCH RIGHT. This will require effort and repetition but he'll catch on faster because of the earlier lesson. Follow the same procedure in teaching him to hunt left, but be prepared for some confusion. Persistent repetition and praise will overcome his doubts.

Then put it all together in daily sessions with combinations of two marked and one blind, and two blind, and finally three blind retrieves. Give a refresher course every time you take him to the field. Firing a shot for the blinds should make the dog more eager and interested at first. The final test is the cold blind in which no shot is fired and no bird is seen to fall by the dog. Increasing the distance and working in higher cover will provide a measure of the dog's acceptance of his training, as will changing the wind direction repeatedly on the blinds. He'll scent birds faster on into-the-wind or crosswind plants, and will hunt out deeper, automatically, on the downwind plants. These routines can be useful in training any gun dog to make accurate blind retrieves.

Blind Water Retrieves

After Junior becomes proficient in marked single and multiple water retrieves and learns to handle blinds on land, teaching him to handle blind retrieves in water will be easier. Begin this routine with either a dead pigeon or the retrieving buck placed in the water by the assistant in a boat or from a point of land across the water from the dog's working area. Put the dog at heel and give him a directional line to the bird with the left arm followed by the command FETCH.

Let's hope he takes a straight line to the bird. If he marks short, a throwing motion with the right arm and the command BACK (already learned on land) should get him out to the bird. If he hunts short and circles, a small rock tossed near the bird, so he can see the splash as the handler commands BACK, BACK, BACK, will get him to the fall. Whistle him in, insist that he deliver while sitting without shaking, and repeat the routine. Since a retriever loves the water and fetching, he should be completing blind water retrieves directed by hand signals and the command BACK up to 75 or more yards by his fourth or fifth training session. In the first lessons a shot fired from a boat or point of land will increase his interest and desire. But he should learn to enter and follow the direction given in a STRAIGHT line to the fall without a shot. And if worked enough he will acquire the confidence to do it. Never fool him. Always give direction correctly and be sure there is something to retrieve when he arrives at the fall.

Teaching the Dog to Go Right or Left to the Fall in Water

As on land it's more difficult for the dog to learn turning and working at a 90 degree angle, right or left, than to swim out farther to reach a fall. A good way to begin this lesson is to set up a downwind blind with dead pigeon and a mark fall forty yards out with the blind

Another mallard is splashed down by one of the hunters. Both claim it after Suzy swims out to fetch and climbs in boat on her return.

Suzy, a good Labrador duck dog, picks up the dead duck but has to swim around the point into a small bay to catch the cripple. Here she comes in with the bird after a long swim.

150

to the left from the marked fall. After Junior has completed the marked retrieve, send him back into the water on the same line he took to the marked bird. When he is the proper distance out, give him one sharp blast on the whistle. When he turns to look at you give him a direction with the left arm EXTENDED and the command Junior LEFT. Repeat the command several times if necessary with arm stabbed in the direction of the bird. Continued effort with this exercise will obtain the desired results. It will require more than a half-dozen successful retrieves to ground him firmly in the desired response.

Follow the same procedure in teaching him to go to the right. Make an effort to have the blind fall downwind from the line he will take to the marked fall so that the scent of the blind will not pull him from his line on the marked retrieve.

Finish out his education for both land and water blind retrieves by a dozen sessions devoted exclusively to blind retrieving. As he progresses and becomes more proficient in going right and left, the handler should include a number of straight-away blinds in the routine so that the dog learns to accept direction to the right, the left, or dead ahead. Since directions to the right or the left will be used by a hunter mostly to correct a faulty mark, it is suggested that 65% of the training here be on straight lines and only 35% on the right and the left. Giving Junior the one-blast SIT whistle in the water is necessary to get his attention to see hand signals. However, if overdone, he may acquire the bad habit of swimming out a few yards and stopping to look back for help. Conditions vary, but if and when this first occurs give him no help and let him search out the area until he finds the bird. Looking back for help voluntarily, which some field trialers call "popping," is an unproductive, unattractive behavior in a retriever gun dog.

Breaking at Water

At some stage Junior is going to hit the water under full throttle without waiting for the command, and compound his felony by ignoring whistle and voice commands to return. There are several corrective measures, the most effective of which is to beat him to the object to be retrieved. Handlers over thirty years old may find this slightly difficult. However, a quick shot in the rump with a marble propelled by a slingshot or with a small, soft shooting Daisy air rifle will often get his attention so that he may be called back to the bank for some harsh words. If it recurs, increase the punishment which should end the problem. If it does not, go back to the yard and roll some shackled pigeons at Junior from a few yards out and by voice and action let him know that he is in extreme peril if he moves. Then return to the water and toss out three or four shackled pigeons, which the handler will retrieve as Junior remains sitting on the bank. Be persistent and don't give up. Convince Junior you mean business.

Training for Spectacular Water Entrance

Field trialers and some hunters want their retrievers to leave the ground when they charge the water and become airborne like Evel Knievel. Many retrievers do this automatically while others slip into the water like a frogman on a wartime mission. To increase enthusiasm for water entrance, work the dog off a three or four-foot bank too steep for him to descend except by jumping. It will work with some dogs, but we know a fine Arkansas duck dog that will run down the shore several hundred yards to find a sloping bank where she can slip in like a fox rather than jump. Her owner does not like it, but puts up with it because she retrieves and seldom loses any ducks and doves each year doing it her way. Perhaps early training would have corrected her fox-like water entry.

Teaching the Dog to Work through Decoys

Place one or two decoys in shallow water near the shore and toss out a canvas buck or dead bird to one side. Junior may try to retrieve one or both decoys when first exposed to them. If he learned the command NO in early yard training, he can probably be persuaded to leave the decoy and complete the retrieve. A dozen retrieves coupled with the voice command NO should get the message over, especially if he has the added inducement of a shackled, live pigeon flapping in the water to attract him. If not, perhaps one shot from a slingshot or air rifle will discourage him. Next, increase the number of decoys in the water and toss the buck so that he will swim close to one as he goes for the bird. Eventually he will get hung up on a decoy anchor line and get back to shore dragging a decoy or two with great effort. A dog of average intelligence will learn to avoid swimming through the spread of decoys if given some encouragement to swim around it after he has been hung up a few times. This is simply a case of the dog learning cause and effect through trial and error. He will learn it if given enough exposure and a refresher session or two the day before the duck season opens.

The Use of Dog's Name with Certain Commands

Many trainers teach their dogs to respond to a short one word command for the logical reason that it's easier for a dog to learn and remember one convenient word rather than two or more. There are times when hunters in the field, yard or blind may be involved with two or more dogs—their own or one or more belonging to a hunting partner. So it's handy to be able to command Junior to kennel up and Jack to heel, and to have both obey, or Junior to retrieve and Jack to stay put. Using the dog's name as a prefix with certain commands like STAY, FETCH, HEEL, KENNEL UP, etc., is a useful tool for hunters working a brace of retrievers, bird dogs or spaniels. And a good place to begin this education is at feeding time with two or more dogs. Command them to SIT, STAY, or HUP, then release them to the feed pan by commands Junior HI ON. Then Jack HI ON, and finally Belle HI ON will teach them to wait for their special, individual orders. However, older dogs will often become sagacious enough to respond to several commands for the same action if worked with and handled enough.

The trainer who has only one dog can often get up training sessions with friends or dog club members in his vicinity to educate two or more dogs to respond to commands given only by their respective trainers or, in case of bracework, by beginning the routine in the yard. If the name is to be a prefix for commands, then use it beginning in the yard work and as suggested at feeding time.

When the puppy is six months old, sit him ten yards from another dog—preferably an older, fully-trained individual. Then alternate single buck retrieving between the two. The puppy can be restrained on lead at first until he learns that he can only retrieve when he hears his name followed by the command FETCH. When this step has been mastered, switch to tossing a few shackled pigeons for a lesson or two, then shoot pigeons on land and ducks at water with the dogs sitting twenty yards apart. Junior should learn this one fast, and it will make him more eager.

By the time he is approaching a year and a half in age, the dog has learned most of the things that can be taught in simulated hunting exercises and training routines if his trainer has seriously

Ron Branaman sits Lucky at the shore line and fires a blank pistol before tossing out the canvas buck. *Goodall*

Lucky has entered the water on command, seized the buck and is now returning to shore on a whistle command. *Goodall*

As she leaves the water Lucky is urged to deliver the buck to hand before shaking off the excess water. *Goodall*

worked at the job. However, a finished retriever must learn the action and smart tricks of wild game before he is truly a finished hunting dog. To top off his "book learning" and expand his ability to cope with the traits and tricks of wise old cocks and drakes, he needs much hunting. He may be slightly confused the first time a crippled wild drake dives just as he is about to be caught. But he'll learn to circle and tread water with high head waiting for the duck to pop *his* head up. And the first time a crippled duck disappears under an overhanging bank it may throw him off slightly until he discovers that a short cruise up and down the bank will reveal her presence to his searching nose. After he has puzzled out the presence of a wise old cock pheasant hiding under wind-rowed rice straw in California, or in a heavy stand of horseweeds in a South Dakota, hog-tight fence corner, or a New England stone fence row, he'll be on his way to becoming a fine, complete and finished retrieving dog. His proud owner-trainer will be displaying pictures of "the best damn retriever in this state" to his friends at the gun club or local sporting goods store. And who can blame him? Because a home-trained gun dog is living proof of most of the great claims his owner-trainer makes about him!

1985 National Amateur Champion Topbrass Cotton with handler Jackie Mertens and friends. Cotton is owned by Bev and Jeff Finley and Jackie and Joe Mertens. To win the National, Jackie and Cotton had to compete against 87 other retrievers, all of which were Labradors except three which were Goldens.

American Brittany Club's 1985 Dual and National Amateur Field Champion Brandee-Britt's Red Jinx. Owner-Handler Dr. Steven Rudd.

The Gordon Setter National Amateur Shooting Dog Champion Springset Kahua Viper, owned and handled in competition by Jim Hustace of Honolulu. Viper is a solid, classy gun dog with 100 wins in field trials including an All-Breed major American Field Trial.

8

What's Your Game?— Non-Migratory Upland Game Birds

The Bobwhite Quail

The great Bobwhite Quail, which many people consider a super game bird, is found in every state east of the Rockies with larger population south of the Mason-Dixon line. This bird also ranks high on the list of gourmet foods and is one of the few wild game birds whose breast is white meat. This bird's popularity can be measured by the fact that they are second in total harvest (estimated 35,000,000) to the Mourning Dove (50,000,000).

The Bobwhite Quail has much adaptability to environment and can thrive on a variety of foods ranging from small grain seeds to grass and weed seeds and legumes such as lespedeza, beggar weed and black weed. In areas of hardwood timber, he can live well all winter on acorns and black weed seeds or late fruit like persimmons.

Quail are covey birds and will remain in the covey from the day they are hatched until they pair off to breed at maturity. They are persistent breeders and will try to nest and hatch a clutch of eggs even if the nest and eggs are destroyed by varmints a half dozen times.

The Bobwhite Quail are edge birds and spend much time in edges of standing grain, stubble and weed field cover or brushy fence rows. They rest, dust, and sun in such spots when not feeding or on the roost.

Pointing dogs are the popular choice for Quail hunting because of their free hunting method and searching action from birdy objective of brushy fence row to another birdy objective or edge of timber. When they cross the line of scent left by a moving covey, they will trail with high head and whip into a point when close enough to take body scent. When the birds are flushed by the hunter and a bird or two is on the ground, some bird dogs are more interested in finding the singles or a new covey than in retrieving the shot bird. When this occurs, it is time to demand that Rover search for the dead and crippled birds by ordering him sternly, DEAD—DEAD—DEAD.

When birds in a large covey are retrieved, most hunters will head for the spot the flushed covey landed. Good hunters will seldom take more than three or four birds, then move on and search for a new covey.

When one or more hunters work two pointing dogs at the same time, one is usually a wide hunter and the other a closer worker. Often the wide dog will find the most coveys. When he does, the other dog must always honor by backing (pointing the dog which made the find). Failing to back can lead to trouble immediately if the one dog attempts to seal the point and flushes the covey.

A successful Quail hunter must have a half dozen or more places to hunt in order to be able to hunt two or three times each week during the Quail season. One way to locate good hunting areas is to cruise the countryside on a number of occasions early in the morning or an hour or two before sunset and count the number of male Quail whistling "Bobwhite." Several whistling cocks probably indicate that there will be several coveys in the area. Making inquiry from rural mail carriers, country store operators, game wardens, and farmer friends can help in finding places to hunt. A small gift to the farmer and his wife is good public relations. Giving them part of the game shot on their farm is better public relations.

The Quail population can climb or descend rapidly on a season of good or bad weather. An icy winter and hot, dry or over-wet summer can reduce the Quail population. However, the persistent effort to nest where they will hatch a clutch of eight to twelve eggs each year enables them to make a comeback after a year of bad weather. Another asset which helps Quail survive is the fact that the cock bird helps with the nesting and raising of the chicks. He will spend time daily on the nest while the hen feeds. If she is killed by a hawk or farmer's house-cat, the cock bird will take over and raise the chicks.

It is said that "Bobwhite Quail hunting and eating are sport and food fit for a king." With more than forty years exposure to each, we most heartily agree.

The Pheasant

The Pheasant population in the United States is probably a blend of stock from northern Caucasus, Mongolia and China. They were grain eaters in their native lands and have continued in that direction in the United States. Their original habitat consisted of flat land, rolling country and foothills usually adjacent to grain fields. They were seldom found in timber according to a survey and study conducted by the Illinois History Survey. We also believe this is true of the Pheasant in the United States, because the only time we have found them in timber was when the ground was covered with deep snow. Pheasant in the United States, unlike their English cousins, roost on the ground, whereas the species in England may roost in trees.

The use of both flushing dogs and pointing dogs in Pheasant hunting is a result of breed loyalty on the part of pointing dog owners who have never hunted or shot over Springer Spaniels or Retrievers when Pheasant hunting. When the flushers take body scent they dive in and drive a Pheasant into instant flight. A large percent of the time, when a pointing dog points a cock Pheasant, the gaudy rascal will sneak away although a hen, illegal in most states, will often lie for the point. We suggest flushing dogs are Pheasant specialists just as pointing dogs are Bobwhite Quail specialists. We never want our good Quail dogs to even see a Pheasant, because he cannot hypnotize the Pheasant like he can the Quail.

Pheasant and Quail like protective cover and in the grain belt often feed in standing corn or beans. Like Canada Geese, they can remove the grains from an ear of corn without disturbing the shuck. One successful system in hunting birds in standing corn is to join forces with several other hunters, walk some five yards apart, then drive the birds to the end of the field. During the drive, it is better to keep the flushing dogs at heel until within forty or fifty yards of the terminal fence row at end of the field. The dog will flush one or maybe several birds, which may give the drivers or the blockers at the end of the field a shot. One or more blockers at the end of the field is necessary when the first bird is flushed, as it is often out of the drivers' range and the only opportunity to harvest that bird may be in the blocker.

When hunting sweet clover, weed field or uncut hay fields where Pheasant also spend time, the flushing dog is ordered to beat and quarter the ground in a favorable wind direction, before right or left quarter. The cock birds will run much less than in corn, but will often try to squat down and let dog and hunter walk past. If successful, they will flush from the hunter's rear and give a "horse laugh" cackle at the stupidity of dog and hunter. A quick snap shot, before the bird is out of range, may change his tune permanently.

In stubble field with adjacent pasture land, Pheasant will often take a quick dash to the cover of the fence row hoping to avoid detection and may lie well for any dog, since cover is limited and scarce. We like to hunt thirty yards downwind from such fence rows, forcing the dog by whistle or voice to quarter out from fence rows. This prevents his dashing down the fence row cover which a smart dog will do if not controlled by voice or whistle. Control the dog by insisting that he quarter with fence row on one side and open field on the other. This is a successful way to take a bird or two from scant cover in just a few minutes.

When a few days of the opening Pheasant season have elapsed, the wily old cock birds will sometimes search out a typical cover like a swamp edge and hop from hummock to hummock when dog and hunter approach. However, a Springer or Retriever will put him in the air and eventually save the hunter's shooting reputation by tracking down the wing-tipped birds which the hunter should have harvested cleanly instead of crippling.

Pheasant hunting along with Bobwhite Quail and rabbit provide most of the non-migratory upland bird and game hunting in the United States.

The Pheasant population is well dispersed in the United States. All they need is habitat and food. We have found and hunted them successfully in Pennsylvania and west through Michigan, Wisconsin, Illinois, Nebraska, Minnesota, the Dakotas, and eastern Colorado. On the west coast we hunted Pheasant in Washington, Oregon, Northern and Southern California, down to the El Centro on the Mexican border and near the Colorado River. School principals in the Dakotas, like the kind-hearted, sportsminded school administrators in some sections of Arkansas, are inclined to not take the roll during Pheasant season in the Dakotas and deer season in Arkansas.

Ruffed Grouse

We have hunted only the Ruffed Grouse and must therefore limit our discussion to this bird which is one of the eighty or more species most widely distributed in the United States and we believe the most popular with hunters. We have hunted the Ruffed Grouse in Michigan and Wisconsin, Colorado and Pennsylvania using both flushing and pointing dogs and have found both types effective Grouse producers. Since they spend much of their time in timber or open grasslands with knee-high cover where it may be difficult to keep track of a pointing dog, it is helpful to bell the pointing dog which should be a close worker. When the bell stops tinkling it usually indicates a point. The flushing dog seldom needs a bell since he is trained to work within gun range. He has a decided edge on pointing breeds in superior retrieving ability and ability to track down cripples. It is exciting and much easier to keep track of a flushing dog as he searches out the area of brush in evergreen timber with his back and forth hunting motion. When his head flies up and his buzzing tail doubles in speed we know a Grouse, tucked in the cover, will soon be airborne with the flusher grabbing for his tail feathers.

Grouse in timber appear to have a special talent which enables them to use a tree like a basketball player uses a pick to avoid the bird shot. We believe such tactics have given the Grouse a slight edge over our shooting. However, we always send the dog to retrieve and hopefully the Retriever or Springer will return with a live cripple on more occasions than our English Setters or Pointers. We add a disclaimer that this opinion is not based on breed loyalty. The English Setter is our favorite gun dog and holds a slight edge over the Labrador, Golden or Springer in our affection, although we think highly of all or most gun dogs. Grouse hunting is truly one of the great sports which is much more exciting and productive when shared with a trained flushing dog or pointing dog. Even a youngster in his first year of hunting will fill your game bag if you are patient, regardless of whether it is a flusher or pointing dog. We prefer the flusher and know we won't have to be yelling and whistling throughout the day to control him or search for him when he is lost on point or has departed for another section of the area, which can happen in Grouse country cover.

161

The Western Quail

There are seven exotic color species of Western Quail which often are undecided on whether to run or fly. This confusion may be transferred to good, honest Bobwhite Quail dogs which specialize in shocking game birds into lying immobile. The dog will improve with proper handling and treatment, but the Western Quail just won't lie before the point of a good bird dog like their distant cousin, the Bobwhite Quail. One or more of the Western Quail inhabit the western states extending from Colorado. They are colorful birds some with head plumes and a liking for desert habitat. Some act almost like domestic chickens. We have seen them one block from downtown Palm Springs, on the campus of Stanford University and dusting in the Mexican sun near the edge of a highway. When we first observed their reluctance to flush, we wondered why hawks, fox, coyote, and other carnivores did not wipe them out, but we learned that two million of the Valley and California Quail had been harvested in one year. They were as wily and wary as the Bobwhite and other native game birds!

The Valley and California Quail

The Valley Quail and the California Quail are so similar we will treat them as the same species although some ornithologists consider them as two species. Although they like timber along the edge of desert valleys with lots of chapparal and sagebrush, we have seen them on the campus of Stanford University and on grassy side streets in Palm Springs where they appear to be much at home dodging house cats and small boys with sticks. They are the most popular of the desert Quail probably because they lie well for a pointing dog. They are available in greater quantities than the other Western Quail and have a head plume topped with a button pointing forward. Their range is up and down the west coast from Washington to Southern California. They also spill over into Nevada and Arizona. Hunters look for them in areas where they can feed on the seed of local vegetation, small grain and some insects. One source estimates the annual average harvest at two million birds. We believe that either a flushing dog trained to quarter his ground, or a close working pointing dog can satisfy most hunters. The flushing dog must quarter and the pointing dog must be a close worker.

While it is true that these birds may lie for a point, they won't hold for a half hour or more like the Bobwhite Quail. The pointing dog who is a close worker "checks in" every few minutes when he loses sight of his hunter/handler.

Gambel's Quail

The Gambel's Quail is similar in appearance to the Valley/California species with a head plume which leans forward when the birds are stationary. They prefer the desert habitat of California, Nevada, Arizona and Colorado where they find buds, fruits and insects available. Their behavior of running to hide when approached is an indication that the hunter with a flushing dog which quarters within gun range, will do a better job than the hunter with a pointing dog. Finding a covey, pointing it and having it move rapidly away from the point when the bird dog is ordered to relocate, won't encourage the dog to remain staunch when he is exposed to such actions repeatedly. It takes a persistent retriever to search out the shot and cripple in dry air and natural desert camouflage. We recommend the flushing dog for these runners.

The Mountain Quail

This bird, which likes foothills and mountain slopes, is crowned with a single straight feather, which points upward unless he is running or flying. His habitat is in country he likes, the coastal states of Washington, south to California and east to Idaho and Nevada. Their habitat suggests a scanty food supply, but these birds thrive on it. Local hunters use both pointing dogs and flushers, but we prefer the flusher because of the birds' reluctance to flush. They prefer to fly downhill. It's easy to shoot over a bird losing altitude, as most hunters are used to game birds which climb skyward when flushed. One famous foreign gun maker formerly produced guns which fired slightly above the target in recognition of the fact that most game birds do climb instead of dropping like the mountain birds. Birds shot while flying downhill will drop farther away from the hunter and his dog. If the dog fails to find a dead or cripple quickly, he may do so if cast farther out than a normal fall of fifteen to twenty-five yards. We liked these sporty birds after we learned to compensate for their downhill flight.

The Harlequin Quail

The Harlequin Quail is a native of Mexico and only occasionally found in the border states. This is not too great a disappointment to United States hunters raised on Bobwhite Quail and Pheasant in the central and eastern areas of the United States. This little fellow is also known as the Mearn's Quail and Fool's Quail since he is more than likely to sit and ignore an approaching hunter. I suppose one could work this bird with any breed of dog. If one of my Springers or Labradors scented this bird, Mr. Fool's Quail would have to flush fast. If he ran, a flushing dog would grab him. My bird dogs, or maybe yours too, would point the bird and stay on point until the bird walked away. In that case, the bird dog would probably grab him and retrieve him to hand.

The Scaled Quail

This bird is also a resident of Mexico but drifts farther across the border than the Harlequin, with range in Arizona, New Mexico, and West Texas. In Texas and perhaps elsewhere, he is known as the Blue Quail and prefers to run rather than fly. But a flushing dog can make this bird, which usually moves around in small coveys of ten or twenty birds (maybe larger numbers in Winter). We have seen this bird and the Harlequin Quail in Mexico and hunted them both, just to learn about them. They are not very sporty and neither will they give us or a good pointing or flushing dog much challenge.

The Grey Partridge

The Grey Partridge, commonly known in the United States as the Hungarian Partridge, was not successfully introduced from Middle Europe until shortly before the turn of the century. He has not propagated in the United States as fast as he did in Canada because he prefers a cooler climate. However, they are found in Wisconsin, Minnesota, and the Dakotas and on to the coast, spreading into Oregon. There are a few scattered pockets in Michigan and perhaps Western New York. These birds are grain eaters. They feed on grain they find in stubble fields and practically any kind of grain will do. We have hunted them with both pointing and flushing dogs in Wisconsin and always found them in picked corn or combined wheat and oat stubble fields. On one occasion, when driving south through central Wisconsin, we saw perhaps 150

"Huns" feeding in a dozen grain fields after a light snow. They were as thick as black birds. In some corn fields their dark color stood out like small crows. They were also in grain stubble fields when we hunted them and flushed ahead of both pointing dogs and Retrievers. On several occasions we were joined by three hunters and all entered the field, which contained perhaps 35 or 40 birds, from a different corner. This system worked in part, but only one hunter got any shooting. When flushed, the birds fly fast and low, set their wings and coast into an adjoining stubble field. Professional trainers who take a string of bird dogs to Canada each summer tell us the young "Huns," Grouse, and Prairie Chickens lie fairly well in cover for pointing dogs. They are fine eating birds and are well larded with fat in the autumn.

The Chukar Partridge

This fine European bird, which was first propagated and liberated in the United States just before the turn of the century, spread up and down the coastal mountains in Washington, Oregon and California. In recent years, it has been released in other states in the East. These attractive fine eating birds are basically grain eaters when they can find it near their rocky terrain, but actually depend on weed seeds and grasshoppers when grain is not available. We hunted them in Oregon with both flushers and pointing dogs and had more luck filling our game bag with a Springer and a big, tough, black Labrador. Here is a quote from a story concerning Chukar Field Trials in Idaho, from the *American Field:*

> Southern Idaho is blessed with some of the best Chukar hunting in the U.S. It separated the (pointing) dog with stamina and desire from the plug shooting dog. Our trial grounds near Jordan Valley supports a native population of Chukar, Hungarian Partridge, Quail and Sage Grouse. Dogs must have desire and drive to work the hills, the cliffs, and the rocks.

This description is most accurate of Chukar territory and that is why the club which schedules trials here has turned out great Chukar champion bird dogs for ten consecutive years. The only thing we can add to this report is Chukar Partridge hunting is not for sissies or dogs which would rather lie by the fire.

Some of the public and private shooting clubs in the United States are advertising availability of Chukar along with Pheasant, Bobwhite Quail and Mallard Ducks. All such clubs use hand-raised birds to release for customers and/or members.

The Mourning Dove

The estimated annual harvest of Mourning Doves reaches 50 million in an average year according to Joel Vance of the Missouri Conservation Department. We can add that it probably accounts for a greater number of dead birds left in the field. Most Dove hunters do not have a retrieving dog to find the dead and crippled birds they drop in standing corn, bean fields or ponds, rivers and lakes where the Doves swing in for a drink. We have not hunted Doves in all or even half of the 39 states which permitted Dove shooting in 1984, but have hunted in enough areas and states, including Mexico. There it is a rare and unusual event to see a Dove hunter using a Retriever or Springer Spaniel flushing dog to retrieve the birds he and his party of shooters drop. We think that is a shame, because we can fully endorse the opinion of the late Bob Beeker, Outdoor Editor of the Chicago Tribune, who made a study of Dove hunting and reported that the few hunters who used Retrievers or Springer Spaniels collected 96% of the birds shot, whereas dogless hunters left better than 50% in the field because the best shooting often occurred in fields of standing grain which had not been harvested. We suggest that if all Dove hunters used dogs to find the shot Doves, it would reduce the total national bag by 30 or 40 percent. Trained dogs do conserve game.

Many Dove hunters have complained to us that they spent five or six hours in the field on opening day and came home with only a few or no birds. Obviously they did not plan their shoot because good Dove hunting is available in 39 of the 50 states for those with a game plan.

The time to make a game plan is soon after the 15th of August in those states where the shooting season opens on September 1. Several early morning or late afternoon trips to the farming areas of their home community will reveal some grain fields and stubble fields like milo, corn, soybeans, oats, wheat, sunflowers or millet where the birds are feeding in quantities before 10:00 A.M. or after 3:00 P.M. Once several such fields are located, the hunter and friends will be set for three or four good shoots for each field if they hunt the area only over three or four days. Several shooters will keep the birds flying, whereas one, even with a flushing dog to move them, may have difficulty taking a legal bag limit.

Mourning Doves follow a set pattern on normal days. They come off the roost shortly before sun-up and head out in bunches of

2, 3 or 20 for a grain or stubble field. If none are available, there won't be many Doves, but those available are locals that nested in the areas and will be heading for weed fields containing black weeds, pine seeds, goat weeds and a hundred others. In the South there are often two or split seasons if the state desires to split up the hunting days allowed by U.S. Fish and Wildlife. Peanuts, sorghum and cowpeas are favorite Dove foods in the South.

In addition to being harvested in greater quantities than any other non-waterfowl U.S. game bird, they make a fast recovery when Nature or Man depletes the population in any one year. Doves nest several times each year and the young mature fast, leaving the nest some 16 days after hatching. Thirty days later, they have feathered out fully. Seventy percent die from natural causes the first year, so conservation departments in most states believe it is better to let hunters take them. Hunters like Doves because of their fine eating qualities. They also like them because these fast flying feathered bombs can increase a shooter's skill in pass shooting and quickly convince any hunter that lots of lead is necessary to bring down a speedy Mourning Dove. The best Dove dogs by far are any of the retriever breeds or the English Springer Spaniel. A hunter backed up against a hedge fence, large oak tree or other cover with a retrieving dog at heel, can often tell when incoming birds are approaching by listening for the rattle of the dog's tail in leaves or patches of cover. He will wag it furiously when he spots incoming Doves or maybe even a Woodpecker or Lark, once he learns what the hunt is all about. And we repeat, a good retrieving dog will conserve game by finding all the dead and crippled birds instead of leaving 50% of them in the field as does the dogless hunter.

The White-winged Dove

This sporty cousin of the Mourning Dove is only found in the states bordering on Mexico, plus Nevada. These five states are the only ones which have an open season on these birds and account for an average bag record of 195,000. We believe this is a reasonably accurate estimate for the national harvest.

White-wings are hunted the same way in both the United States and Mexico as the Mourning Doves. In states where there are both Mourning Doves and White-winged Doves they often roost in the same general area. In the morning, the White-wings leave the roost first, followed by the Doves perhaps an hour later. In the evening, the White-wings finish feeding, watering and dusting before the Mourning Doves and go to roost first. As food, we cannot distinguish between them as both have dark meat breasts and when roasted or baked correctly are delightful. Several hunters should surround a field where either species is feeding and, after taking their daily limit, let the field rest for several days in order not to drive the birds to other areas. We highly recommend that White-wing shooters use dogs trained to retrieve. Such a dog will conserve game by finding all the dead and crippled birds.

The American Woodcock

The American Woodcock is a fine, long-billed, worm-eating game bird often called a Timberdoodle by hunters. This sporty game bird spends the summer breeding season in 35 states north of the Mason-Dixon line in the Atlantic and Mississippi Flyways, only four (Kansas, Nebraska, Oklahoma and Texas) in the Central Flyway and none in the Pacific Flyway. This short-tailed, large-eyed bird winters in southern states from Florida in the East to Texas in the West. Since he is a long-billed worm-eater, he must remain south of the frost line to survive. Obviously his long bill dictates his habitat and eating habits, so he always remains close to wetlands adjacent to timber and edges of sloughs located in or near timber.

We have often found Woodcock with our flushing or pointing dogs when the birds are moving south by easy stages in Bobwhite Quail country. Before they head south we have found them in timber wetland adjacent to Grouse habitat in Wisconsin and Michigan and elsewhere. During the summer, just 45 miles from the Chicago Loop, we located a dozen nesting spots for Woodcock. We worked and developed some good Woodcock dogs of both pointing and flushing variety in these northern Illinois areas before and after the nesting season. Occasionally, when Indian Summer weather arrived before frost time, we could take not more than two limits of birds to really test the dogs on the real thing. None of our dogs ever refused to pick up and deliver to hand the first Woodcock they were sent to fetch. But all of our dogs were obedience trained to retrieve as described in the sections of this book on training gun dogs to retrieve.

We believe that New England and other Eastern bird hunters spend more time hunting Woodcock than do Middle-Westerners.

New England is really the heart of the Woodcock country in the United States, with the population declining as one heads west. We have hunted them in Minnesota, Wisconsin, Michigan and Pennsylvania early in the autumn. We moved down to southern Illinois and Arkansas to harvest a mixed bag of Quail and Woodcock before we settled down to hunt Bobwhite Quail exclusively with pointing dogs which we have worked into condition. It is always rather amusing to observe a Quail hunting buddy break up the first time our quail dogs point out Woodcock during a hunt. The Woodcock is tied with the Jack Snipe for top performer of gamebird acrobatics. His antics are a butterfly-like flight, now towering, now dipping, then rising again above the tree tops, he swings in a wide circle and often returns to the spot from which he flushed. They are fine table birds and we have hunted them with both pointing and flushing dogs. We prefer the flusher since he always works within gun range without much handling, whereas the pointing dog, even a close worker, really needs to be belled and searched-for when the bell stops ringing.

The Band-tailed Pigeon

The Band-tailed Pigeon bears a strong resemblance to the common pigeon officially named the Rock Dove which is a resident of every U.S. farmer's barn and the streets of towns and cities of Mexico. They have a tendency to breed and summer in the states of Washington, Oregon, California, Nevada, Utah, Colorado, New Mexico and Arizona. A surprising number of hunters in these states bought duck stamps (20,000 harvested 136,000 birds).

We have seen the birds and observed hunters working them with dogs in California and actually hunted them in Mexico where they exist in great quantities and are called "Blue Pigeons." Like the Mourning Doves and White-winged Doves, the Pigeons are grain and seed eaters and roost in trees, including palm trees. They feed and sometimes flock with the two species of Doves and perhaps roost with or near them. They are slower flyers than the Doves and seldom flock together in larger bunches than five or six. They are successfully hunted exactly like Doves and just as difficult to find when shot. We urge Dove hunters to have an English Springer Spaniel or Retriever when they hunt pigeons. This will eliminate the wasteful loss of the dead and cripples. We have had a few hunts of these fine eating birds in northern California.

The Common Snipe

The Common Snipe, also called the Jack Snipe, is tied with the Woodcock for first place as the leading game bird acrobat. In flight he looks like a wing-ed golf ball carrying its own tee. He loves to travel spending summer in the northern third of the United States, up through most of Canada. The winter sees him in the lower half of the United States, down through Mexico to all of Central America. Duck Stamp buyers reported having harvested Snipe in every state of the Union, including Alaska. Hunters should walk in groups of two or three on the edge of water ranging from farm ponds to large lakes and rivers with low growth vegetation and mud flats. Snipes like rice fields and drainage ditches. When flushed, he repeats a "scape-scape" whistle, zigzags up, does a wingover and often returns to the spot from which he was flushed. He is reluctant to hold for a point and often flushes wild for a flushing dog, but when he circles back gives the hunter a second shot and often requires a Retriever or Springer to find the shallow water where he feeds on small invertebrates. His average weight of four or five ounces requires several birds to feed a hungry hunter. Flushing dogs are the best Snipe dogs by far.

1984 Estimated Harvest of Migratory Upland Game
Exclusive of Waterfowl

Species	Duck Stamps Purchased	Total Harvest
Mourning Doves	480,000	11,315,200
White-winged Doves	15,300	184,600
Band-tailed Pigeons	20,100	131,600
American Woodcock	135,400	482,200
Common Snipe	55,700	380,200
Sandhill Crane	9,900	16,800
Sora Rail	4,600	26,400
Other Rails	10,700	82,500
Gallinules	5,100	47,100

9

What's Your Game?— Migratory Waterfowl and Rabbits

T HE TREK SOUTH each autumn by millions of waterfowl is an exciting time for the 1,768,300 hunters who purchase duck stamps and those misguided poachers who don't. Fortunately some of the poachers get caught and lose their guns and a heavy chunk of cash. Their cash, along with $6,000,000 in annual contributions by the sporting efforts of Ducks Unlimited, National Wildlife Federation, Izaak Walton League and members of other sporting and civic organizations, furnishes much of the financing for wildlife management. The management and conservation measures in the so-called duck factory of the Canadian grain and pothole country, keep flocks of ducks and geese moving south through the four great U.S. flyways, by the millions, each autumn. The lovely wild call of the Canada and Snow Geese high in the sky on a full moonlight night, causes half a million retrievers and Springer Spaniel duck dogs to whine and shiver with excitement, anticipating the pleasure of fetching warm, feathered bodies from the chilly waters of lakes and rivers or the burr infested, standing grain and stubble fields where birds do their feeding.

The four great flyways have been the roads for the round trip of migrating waterfowl since the slow retreat of the great glaciers.

Going from east to west they are; the Atlantic, the Mississippi, the Central and the Pacific. There is also a mini-flyway in Alaska. The traffic in each of the flyways changes annually depending on climate conditions in the spring and summer and in the fall when the birds head south.

Nature plays no favorites in that several million ducks and more than four hundred thousand geese are harvested in each flyway except the Pacific, and the mini flyway in Alaska. Nature's generosity does not stop there because the Canada Goose and the Mallard Duck either nest or winter in every one of the United States. The Mallard Duck is the species which is harvested in the greatest numbers in all flyways except the Atlantic, where Mr. Green Head is second to the colorful Wood Duck. The Canada Goose is the bird harvested in largest quantity in all flyways. (see flyway chart and map)

Sometimes both ducks and geese will change flyways as the experience of a friend can attest. He lives in Rockford, Illinois and in addition to saving all crippled ducks he harvested on the Illinois River, he had friends do the same for him. On several occasions some of his now healthy cripples would switch species when selecting a mate. On one occasion a Bull Sprig (male Pintail) mated with a Mallard hen and one of the offspring switched flyways and headed with a flock up the Atlantic Flyway. Our friend got a letter from a member of a Maine Duck Club during the next hunting season which said, "for Heaven's sake," or words to that effect, "tell us the species of the duck that carries your name, address and tag #909. Two members had a fight after a violent argument in backing their identity of your duck. Let us know, before other members elevate arguments into fist fights."

Waterfowl migration to southern wintering grounds usually begins when short days and cooler weather tell the Teal to head south. The other species follow a week or two behind the Teal. But changes in the weather can change the normal migration pattern completely. In 1940 for instance, an Armistice Day storm caused the birds to leave and continue nonstop to the deep South. The second heavy storm followed them as far south as southern Illinois and eliminated all duck hunting in the north and center of the country.

We remember the day we were Pheasant hunting with two good Springer Spaniels near DeKalb, Illinois. We parked the car and cast the brace of Springers off about 8:30 A.M. The dogs worked well and we soon had a cock Pheasant and two Quail in our hunting coats when the wind suddenly began to blow and the temperature dropped from 50 degrees to 30 degrees in about 15 minutes. It began to rain in torrents. We headed toward our car parked about a mile away, when suddenly a barn door floated in the air and landed near us with a crash. We were soaked to the skin. The rain stopped as quickly as it started, but the wind increased to gale velocity. Both dogs came to heel without a command, with tails tucked between their legs. We got down in a dry irrigation ditch and continued toward the car. Shortly, several rabbits appeared in the ditch, with three Pheasant hens. We walked by them and so did the two Springers. The rabbits and birds ignored us and the dogs did not even give them a glance. After another barn door or two floated over our heads, we reached the car and headed for home. A dozen duck hunters froze to death that night in several Mississippi River Islands and in Wisconsin and Minnesota lots of barn doors and several houses were whisked away by wind and mini-tornados. Ducks and Geese passed through Wisconsin, Illinois and Indiana riding on a tail wind. Middle-western duck hunters put away their guns and boots for the season.

Estimated 1984 Waterfowl Harvest
Reported to the U.S. Fish and Wildlife Service.

Flyway	Duck Stamp Buyers	Duck Harvest	Coot Harvest	Goose Harvest
Atlantic	414,600	1,846,800	26,000	496,500
Mississippi	679,400	565,300	210,100	464,300
Central	330,600	2,184,400	29,800	585,000
Pacific	325,200	2,460,700	63,300	278,500
Alaska Mini Flyway	18,500	89,700	600	7,700

The mini-flyway in Alaska is used exclusively in the winter by those cold weather ducks like Eider, Old Squaw and Harlequin Ducks and a few geese with thermostats which always run hot.

HUNTING MIGRATORY WATERFOWL

The hunter who downs waterfowl on land or water will be able to find it without a dog in 60% or 70% of the cases if it falls in short cover and is not carried away by wind or current. If it is a cripple, the percentage may decrease to zero. The duck hunter should have a dog trained to retrieve (dog will average 98% retrieved), or he may lose two things; the bird or his life. We can never forget the sad death of a friend who waded down to the river end of a sandbar in the Mississippi River to retrieve a shot goose. His last step took him in over the top of his hip boots. He never came up that cold November day and neither did his goose.

The most popular waterfowl retriever is the Labrador Retriever, followed by the Golden Retriever with the Chesapeake Bay Retriever in third place according to a study of American Kennel Club registration figures and entries in Retriever field trials. There can be no doubt that Retrievers are the top water dogs of the United States and England too, so we hear. They have a strong instinct to retrieve, fine cold weather coat with resistance to water and trainable, tractable dispositions. The other Retriever breeds which have an aptitude for water retrieving are the Flat Coated and Curly Coated Retrievers, Irish Water Spaniels and American Water Spaniels. These are much less popular with hunters as indicated by the fact that fewer than 300 of each are registered each year.

The English Springer Spaniel is a good water dog too. Although less than half the weight of the average retriever and with a less water resistant coat, he can become a good duck dog if introduced to cold water gradually in the fall before duck season. We have hunted ducks many times in Crab Orchard Lake, Horseshoe Lake and other waters in southern Illinois and Wisconsin with Springers and Retrievers. We suggest that Retrievers can take sub-freezing temperature better than Springers and will not tire so quickly in cattail sloughs. The Springer can carry a 7-lb. goose without difficulty. On one occasion we used 35-lb. Square Peg, a Springer bitch, on a goose shoot in a pit on the border of Crab Orchard Lake Wildlife Refuge. We had two harvested geese in the pit and two over the fence which was off limits for people but not for dogs. We sent Peg on a cold blind retrieve, through a hole in the fence. She found and retrieved a crippled Mallard Duck which we had not shot. We sent her back and she returned with another Wing-tipped Mallard Duck which we did not shoot. On her third trip, she found a crippled goose which we had shot and retrieved it to hand although that big gander nearly beat her to death with his one good wing. On her fourth trip back, she found a dead, still warm goose which we thought was ours, but bumped into another cripple on her trip in with the dead bird. She fairly spit that dead goose to me and rushed back, without command, for the cripple. Since two was the legal limit per person, we ordered Peg to drop that cripple. Eventually she did so reluctantly and came to heel. As we left the field a game warden flagged us down and said, "How come you boys did not bring in that last goose?" We replied, "It was not our bird and we already had a legal limit." He said, "Good thing that dog is trained, because I watched you through the glasses and so did the Federal Game Warden who was with me. That trained dog kept you two out of jail when she dropped the goose."

Blind or Pit Shooting

When shooting from a shore blind or one perched on stilts high in the water, a peek hole or lower level shelf with 180 degree visibility for the dog should be constructed. Pre-season training of the dog to remain quiet and motionless will pay off. Summer training which teaches the dog to avoid problems by circling the decoys instead of swimming through them is important. When birds are responding to a hale or highball duck call, dogs and hunters should remain quiet and motionless when the birds are circling and looking over the set-up. When they come within range, we think it is more sporting to shoot them in the air rather than let them land and flush before shooting. One cannot predict how and when the next bunch will arrive, but one sure way to attract another bunch is to send the dog to retrieve immediately after shooting. Such action never fails to attract another bunch which flair immediately when they see the dog in the water. It is more productive to wait until several birds are down before sending the dog to retrieve. He may have marked some from his peek hole in the water blinds. But if he has been given lessons on handling and completing cold blind retrieves (no shot— did not see bird fall), he will accept a handler's hand signals, find the downed birds and deliver them to hand. This can transpire after the hunter had a limit on the water during lulls in the action. Young dogs may become bored during half-hour lulls in the action and require some firm words to remain quiet and motionless.

Pass Shooting

Successful pass shooting of waterfowl occurs when pre-season scouting reveals a place where waterfowl move from one area to another. This occurs while they are going or coming from food or

175

rest on their morning flight. Often birds will use the same flight pattern day after day. When such an air path over the same ground path occurs, the hunter and his dog can construct a brush hide on that path and be ready for the next movement of birds. In timber the hunter can back up against a cypress or hardwood tree with the dog closely at heel, with enough protection to get some shooting. Working a duck or goose call is a most useful hunting aid to bring in distant or high flying birds, but usually the action is so fast on a pass shoot that to call or not to call requires judgment and experience. Shooting a pass shoot with rest days in between will keep it active. Shooting it every day may burn it out and send the birds elsewhere.

We have often located good places to pass shoot for future action by carefully observing and scouting after we have limited for the day. When waterfowl are active and flying continuously, one can often limit out in a half hour. That is a good time to look for pass shoot areas and do a little special dog training if necessary. Toss out your diving or trash ducks into a cattail area when the dog is not looking. Handling him to that cold blind fall is a helpful refresher course for a young dog. Hand signals to the right or left with vocal commands to push him out further will reinforce his training. Such time will improve the dog's handling and keep the hunter from that interesting work at home like washing and putting up storm windows or performing household chores.

Jump Shooting

The sporty action of jump shooting is most often done on butterfly days when nothing is flying but Blackbirds, Crows and Woodpeckers. On such days, ducks will often drop into sloughs with head-high cattails and hummocks of firm land sticking up every few feet. Those hummocks are either too close together or too far apart for normal steps and are man killers for both hunter and his dog if the action is slow. When it is fast, it keeps the adrenalin flowing for both hunter and dog so that neither is ready to quit when the limit is reached.

Jump shooting spots are always located near a body of water which overflows or backs up into adjoining lowlands. Smart weeds, duck potatoes, wild rice, wild millet and a hundred other semi-aquatic and water plants grow in such areas. Ducks like such food and will drop into sloughs and marshes which contain these plants. Here they also have some protection from hawks and varmints which like duck meat. It is usually a few individual birds rather than a flock which feed and rest in such areas. Wading through with a flushing dog plowing ahead to flush and retrieve harvested birds is fun and very sporty shooting. If the pheasant season has been open several days, a wily old cock who is trying to avoid hunters may be perched on a hummock. Also a Woodcock may be flushed from the edge. A lone Jack Snipe often feeds in such areas also. Both the hunter and the dog will enjoy the mixed bag of a Mallard or two, several Woodcock and Jack Snipe and a tough old cock Pheasant to give away to a neighbor who does not hunt.

If the slough edges up to a river or creek, paddling the edges with the dog doing the hard work in the slough can be fun too, but it may require a little patience to teach the dog that you are not going to leave him when you move along in the boat. Standing up in a moving canoe or duck boat to shoot a Mallard 40 yards away and flying just above the top of the head-high cover, can be a challenge. We have had to walk downstream in wet clothes to catch up with the canoe when the boat touched on a willow tree and spilled us into the water. Two hours later when we arrived back at the car with wet pants and coat, no dog and no birds, we wondered if it was still fun. But when the Labrador or Springer crawled out from underneath the car, having backtrailed to his ride home, we promised ourselves we would never do it again—until tomorrow, when the ducks failed to show up at our blind and we had to go jump shooting to please the dog.

Green Timber Duck Hunting

Standing in 8 or 10 inches of water which has overflowed from a nearby creek or river, shooting ducks in tall green timber, is not the most popular form of duck hunting. However, it can be exciting, disappointing and a good way to raise the hunter's blood pressure. The exciting part comes when the hunter makes the woods ring with a series of high ball calls interspersed with feeding chuckles and a pair of Mallards beginning to swing down to the big oak and other hardwood trees. The Retriever or Springer gets excited too, whining softly, eyes glued to the sky and the tip of his tongue barely protruding from his mouth. When the birds are near tree-top height and the hunter shoulders his 12 gauge for a quick snap shot, the birds catch the motion, drop their tails and climb rapidly out of range, accompanied by a yelp of disappointment from the dog. The hunter's chagrin wells up into a black cloud of disappointment as the brown leaves float down from the two quick shots he fired at the departing ducks. But this is not the end of the hunt. It has only begun. More calling and a raised arm to calm the dog raise the hunter's blood pressure when a pair of Sprigs dart down below tree top level and fall into the backwater following two quick shots of the 12 gauge. The ducks were attracted by the calling and responded because they like to feed on acorns and want to join the others they hear calling.

One of the famous green timber duck shooting areas in the United States is near Stuttgart, Arkansas. The Arkansas and White Rivers are often at flood stage from fall rains and back up into large tracts of timber. Ducks are attracted to the area by the rice and other grain fields and farm ponds which dot the area. We have hunted there and often move out of the blind or goose pit on a butterfly day to head for flooded timber a few miles away. Most of the ducks in the area will be resting on ponds or lakes or backwaters of the river, but a few will be taking short flights and those are the ones which respond to the calling. We have hunted other green timber areas in southern Illinois in overflow backwater of the Big Muddy River, the Mississippi, Wabash and Ohio Rivers. Sometimes one can take a limit of ducks in a half hour if the dog tracks down, by a swimming search, two Wing-tipped cripples. Eventually he will come up with the cripples and we will pack it in for the day.

There are hundreds of such spots throughout the South where ducks can be taken in green timber if the hunter will take the time to search them out. The action depends to a large extent on the hunter's ability to blow a duck call—especially the hale or highball calls and the feed chuckle. It also helps if the hunter will kick the water noisily to assimilate noise of babbling ducks. Once the dog learns the routine, he will alert the hunter by the noise of his tail beating in the water when a brace of Mallards tries to slip in from the rear. It's fun and fine sport even if the first few shots bring down nothing but a few dead leaves or a limb from a massive oak.

THE BIRDS

The Sandhill Crane

The Sandhill Crane is a long-legged wading bird related to the

Whooping Crane which U.S. Fish and Wildlife Service officials have worked hard to save from extinction. We have never hunted them because we did not think of them as acceptable table birds. However, about 10,000 duck stamp buyers in 10 states report 1984 harvest of the species with an estimated bag of 16,000. Texas and North Dakota alone combined to harvest 13,000. We have walked up a few while hunting Jack Snipe and other game and have seen great flocks of them in Iowa and Nebraska during autumn migration, but have never hunted them. We would expect one of our good quail dogs who had been taught not to work chickens, larks, crows or other non-game birds to ignore Cranes. However, if he did attempt to point a Crane, we suspect it would have to be a sight and not a nose point, because of the tall bird's wide field of vision. We know a good Retriever could fetch one and that he, along with a Springer, would flush one, so we fall back on the ancient cliche which says, "when in doubt use a flushing dog." We know he will get the job done as did his ancestors in seventeenth century England. Spaniels in that day flushed all types of ground birds, including stork and game with hawks and hound.

The Rails

There are ten species of Rails in the United States of which the Sora is the most widely distributed. Also the most popular with hunters, Duck Stamp buyers hunted them in 33 states and bagged a total of 26,000. There were duck stamp buyers in 36 states which hunted the other 9 species and bagged some 80,000, but the Sora is the one that U.S. hunters like most. All Rails are very secretive, spend most of their time hiding, and will fly only when pressed by a bold flushing Springer or Retriever. Few people ever see them because only a handful of dedicated hunters and bird watchers know where to look.

The Gallinule

There are two species of Gallinule with the Common Gallinule occupying most of 33 states. U.S. duck stamp buyers reported bagging an estimated 47,000 in 1984. The Purple Gallinule range is restricted to Florida and the east and west coast of Mexico. We note one authority reported that the species was a poor eating bird, seldom hunted. Apparently that authority failed to consult the U.S.

Fish and Wildlife Service which reported an estimated 6,000 hunters of the bird, half of which were residents of the Mississippi Flyway states with 4,300 in Louisiana. We will fall back on that previously quoted cliche in our recommendation of a gun dog to hunt and retrieve Rail by saying again, when in doubt, use a flusher. To clear up a mystery, Gallinules cannot walk on water. Like the Coot, they half run, half fly when they take off from water. However, when Gallinules walk on lily pads with the help of the "air bags" on their feet, it appears that they are walking on water. Only a fabled Labrador Retriever could do that and he was criticized by the owner's hunting partner for not swimming when he retrieved ducks.

HOW AND WHERE TO HUNT RABBITS

Rabbits, of course, are not birds, but they certainly are upland game. In numbers they are probably the largest species of upland game in the United States, since they are found in every state. There are two genera of rabbits in North and South America; the Volcano Rabbit of Mexico and the Cottontail which is distributed over both North and South America in 13 species and 66 subspecies. The Cottontail is the most highly prized by hunters and represents the largest population. The Swamp Rabbit and the Hare (Jack Rabbit) are also hunted extensively. There are rabbits and predators in every state, including the hawks headed by Blue Darter (Cooper's Hawk) and Goshawk. Rabbits of every species are the number one food item for coyotes, fox and the larger owls.

It has been estimated by outdoor authorities that rabbits are hunted more than any other species of upland game. We think this is probably true since many boys in small towns and on farms begin hunting rabbits with slingshots or pellet guns before graduating to the family shotgun. Illinois did an in depth study of rabbits some years ago and reported the harvest exceeded five million each year from 1956 through 1960. If the other states harvest an average of only 25% of this total, the U.S. total of rabbits harvested would exceed the 50 million Mourning Doves estimated by Joel Vance of the Missouri Conservation Department.

If the large harvest by hunters is coupled with the kill by predators and the loss from disease, it becomes a very large drain on the population each year. How are there any rabbits left as seed breeding stock? Part, if not all of the answer lies in the fact that rabbits breed from February through October each year, raising litters of four to six young five or six times each year. In fact, the buck is waiting near the nest to breed the doe the first time she leaves the nest after dropping her litter. This means another litter will be born about 30 days later, according to the Illinois Natural History Survey. So it appears that there will always be rabbits in every state. As a practical matter of survival, rabbits remain in or near to escape cover most of the day and do a lot of their feeding and frolicking at night. We doubt that any veteran rabbit hunter would disagree with our opinion that hounds are the best rabbit dogs. The small breeds like Beagles and Bassets are the best because they drive the flushed rabbit more slowly than the larger hounds. This means that when flushed, the rabbit usually circles back to his original seat. Since they travel at half-speed to keep ahead of the small hounds, the hunter has a better opportunity to harvest the bunny., However, flushing dogs can provide a lot of sport and harvested rabbits when hunted correctly in cover. We like to move parallel to a bushy fence row on the downwind side with our Springer or Retriever beating back and forth between the fence row and patches of briars or stubble on the downwind side. It is important to keep the dog quartering and not moving straight down the fence row as he may miss much ground coverage and can soon be out of gun range if he moves down the fence row. We want him to reach the fence row every eight or ten yards, since his nose will tell him before he reaches the fence if there is game lurking in the cover. When game is shot, the dog should be sitting or standing at point of flush. If he is not steady to flush and shot, he can disturb a lot of game by chasing the rabbit.

In a weed field it is wise to keep the dog quartering at all times. It is difficult to get a shot off in a heavy weed field, but since rabbits are often hiding in cover, fence rows, standing corn or grain fields are about the only areas that may contain rabbits.

We enjoy the music when a brace of Beagles strikes scent and opens on the line. When their voice changes from trailing to sight running the rabbit, we really don't care if we get a shot or not, as long as the little hounds can continue their sweet hunting music. It is far better than opera or country western music.

Should a hunter work his pointing dogs on rabbit? No, no, a thousand times no. Since there may be more rabbits than game birds in any given field or hunting area, it is most annoying and irritating to walk ahead of a dog on point and flush a rabbit instead of a game bird. And, if a thoughtless hunting partner should shoot a rabbit over a good Quail dog, it may require a lot of time and effort to convince the Quail dog that he is not to point rabbits or other ground game.

An English Setter or Pointer stacked up in a rabbit point is not quite as stylish and lofty as when he points a game bird. We never punish a dog for pointing anything. Instead, we walk away from him calling him to heel as we walk away. Such treatment will usually cure him of pointing rabbits. Do hunt rabbits with a hound or flushing dog, but never with a pointing breed, except on rare occasions. German Shorthaired Pointer owners in Europe use their dogs on both fur and feather and sometimes their U.S. owners do too. Dedicated Quail, Pheasant, Grouse, Woodcock hunters never do.

Mallard

10

Where the Birds Are

THIS CHAPTER IS DESIGNED to provide U.S. hunters with knowledge of the fine effort in conservation and game management by the U.S. Fish and Wildlife Service. It will also provide knowledge of areas which offer the best hunting for several species of upland game and waterfowl.

The management of migratory waterfowl in the U.S. comes under the jurisdiction of the U.S. Fish and Wildlife Service, which is an important division of the Department of the Interior. The management of most other game birds is controlled by the individual states. In order to obtain the most accurate information possible about the distribution of U.S. game birds, we consulted the U.S. Fish and Game and were immediately sent full information by expert game biologist Elwood M. Martin from the Office of Migratory Bird Management.

From the information received, we prepared maps of the four great waterfowl flyways and several charts. The first illustrates the estimated harvest of ducks, geese, and coot, also the duck stamps purchased in each flyway. A second chart illustrates the estimated harvest, by purchasers of duck stamps, of migratory game birds other than waterfowl. We must emphasize that the U.S. Fish and Game Service strongly advises that all harvest records be treated with caution, since they were compiled from questionnaires returned by buyers of duck stamps. Even though all waterfowl hunters are required to purchase duck stamps and return questionnaires reporting the harvest of all game bagged, they are not 100% accurate. They are, however, tools utilized for game management purposes by the Fish and Game Service.

The 1,768,900 duck stamp buyers supplied all the harvest figures. They represent less than 15% of the holders of state hunting licenses, which total 15,500,000. However, the reports of non-waterfowl migratory game birds can provide hunters with adequate information relative to distribution of several species, such as Mourning Doves, Woodcock, Jack Snipe if they multiply the figures listed by six or seven to obtain rough estimates of total U.S. harvest.

Non-Migratory Upland Game Birds

In 1984, 15,500,000 U.S. hunters bought hunting licenses in one of the 50 States, but only 1,768,300 bought Federal duck stamps which are required of all who hunt waterfowl. These figures indicate quite clearly that hunting upland game including the nine species which migrate like the Mourning Doves, Woodcock and Jack Snipe provides the greatest opportunity for U.S. hunters and their several million gun dogs to enjoy this ancient sport.

As a service, we have prepared a map of the four great U.S. migratory flyways for waterfowl and charts listing the estimated harvest figures indicating where the greatest numbers of waterfowl are harvested, and estimated harvest figures of the nine species of upland game birds which also migrate each year. The figures in these charts are based on records and surveys by the U.S. Fish and Wildlife Service. Estimated harvest counts of non-migratory game birds which are managed and controlled by the individual states are more difficult to find, as some states do not keep such records and others are not interested in revealing them to citizens of other states. However, we will reveal the information acquired from libraries and state conservation officials who were most willing to cooperate.

Our chart reveals that the Mourning Dove heads the list of upland game birds with 480,000 hunters who buy duck stamps, harvesting 11 million birds. Joel Vance of the Missouri Conservation Department, estimates that 50 million Mourning Doves are harvested annually. Knowing that doves will breed and nest three to five times each year and are hunted in 39 states with open seasons, we do not find these figures difficult to accept. We have never been able to find a figure for the number of hunters who hunt rabbits, or how many they harvest each year. Since the Cottontail and his cousin, the

184

long-legged Jack Rabbit, are found in every state in the union, and since they breed constantly from February to October five or six times annually, we believe their harvest may exceed that of the Vance estimate for Mourning Doves.

We believe the Bobwhite Quail and the Pheasant attract the most non-migratory game bird hunters and the largest bag limits. Vance estimates that 35 million Bobwhite Quail are harvested each year and supplied us with harvest records for the following states:

Texas	2½ to 3 million	South Carolina	1.4 million
Oklahoma	2.2 million	Alabama & Illinois	
Kansas	2.1 million		1 million each
Florida	600,000	North Carolina	800,000

The Bobwhite Quail

The harvest of the Bobwhite Quail can vary considerably. For instance, the 1984 and 1985 icy winters and wet springs reduced the Quail population drastically in Illinois, Missouri, Kansas, and Arkansas. However, the species usually recovers in a year or two after poor hatching seasons, since the hen will hatch on an average of eight or ten chicks even if she has to replace two or three nests destroyed by predators. Spring is the normal hatching time, but some states report that 40% of the Bobwhite Quail are hatched in August, so the hen will keep trying until she finally succeeds.

Quail are seed and grain eaters, and the coveys use or stay close to the edges of weed fields, or timber, which provides escape cover when not feeding. They often move from one area to another by trailing through fence rows which contain some cover.

The Ringnecked Pheasant

We have no estimates of total harvest or the number of U.S. Ringnecked Pheasant hunters, but ever since these gaudy foreigners were introduced into Oregon's Willamette Valley in 1881, these colorful birds from China have gradually adapted to several types of U.S. terrain and climate. They can be found in all the northern states and are gradually extending their range into states south of the Mason-Dixon line. We have hunted them in Oregon and California north of San Francisco and south to the Mexican border and have seen them in Pennsylvania, Michigan, Wisconsin, Illinois and Minnesota. We know Missouri has introduced them and so have certain areas in Texas. We estimate the Ringnecked Pheasant is just behind the Bobwhite Quail in popularity with hunters. They are grain and seed eaters and hardy birds which can adapt to hot and cold weather with medium good habitat. They are the principal game supplied in private and commercial hunting clubs. Pheasant do not pair off during the breeding season. One cock bird will mate several times with each of five or more hens until they have completed laying a clutch of eight or more eggs. One conservation official gave us an educated guess that Iowa, Kansas, Nebraska and South Dakota each harvested more than a million Pheasant annually. In some states, teenagers are not charged with an unexcused absence by sports-minded school officials on opening day of Pheasant season. In some smaller towns, all businesses close and everyone goes Pheasant hunting.

The Five Species of Grouse

There are five species of game birds which carry the name Grouse. They are the Ruffed, Blue, Spruce, Sage and Sharp-Tailed Grouse. The Ruffed Grouse is found in larger numbers and is more widely distributed in the U.S. than the other members of the Grouse family. The range of the Ruffed Grouse and its several subspecies finds it widely distributed throughout the U.S. mostly along the northern states adjacent to Canada.

It is found in several locations in the Rocky Mountain states down through Colorado then on to Washington, Oregon and several adjacent western states. Perhaps the greatest concentration is in the eastern states and south through Virginia to northern Georgia. They can be found in stands of evergreen trees in the winter and in cover adjacent to hardwood timber in the summer and early fall. We have hunted and found Grouse in cover adjacent to marsh land and where we also found Woodcock.

The Sage Grouse has a liking for sagebrush flat lands and foothills. They range from the Dakotas south to Nebraska, northern California and northwest New Mexico. This bird ranges in some of the Great Plains states, east of the Rocky Mountains, south to New Mexico and as far east as western Minnesota and northern Wisconsin.

The Spruce Grouse, often called "Fool Hen," because of his reluctance to run or flush, ranges from Maine and northern New York, west through states bordering Canada, Washington and

Oregon where ancient Indian tribes also referred to the bird as "Fool Hen."

The Sharp-Tailed Grouse is mostly a western bird which likes plains and prairies. It is found in small quantities in some states west of the Great Lakes.

The Blue Grouse also known as the Dusky Grouse is strictly a western bird. His range is mostly the evergreen timber of the Rocky Mountains and in Colorado, Arizona, Utah, New Mexico and Nevada. This bird is a reluctant flyer and slow to take alarm, which has earned him also the title of "Fool Hen."

Our Grouse hunting experience is limited to the Ruffed Grouse in Pennsylvania, Wisconsin, Colorado, Michigan, and Minnesota. We found them mostly in timber or brush cover adjacent to timber of marshy land which contained Woodcock. Grouse are super eating birds and rank with me just slightly behind Bobwhite Quail and Canvasback Duck.

They are relatively slow flyers but have a unique ability to dodge behind pine trees a half-second after being flushed by a Springer or Retriever or by a hunter who walks one up in front of a pointing dog. They love apple orchards and old farmhouse gardens. They are super game birds which can make the woods roar when the cocks stand on an old hollow log and beat their wings with machine gun speed during spring breeding season.

The Prairie Chicken

The Prairie Chicken is a fine sporty game bird known by ornithologists as the Pinnated Grouse, of which are two sub-species. They are Lesser Pinnated Grouse and Attwater's Pinnated Grouse. The Prairie Chicken, unlike the Ruffed Grouse, prefers the prairie to timber and in the early part of this century existed east of the Rocky Mountains on the Great Plains, in the millions. When their habitat was destroyed by grain farmers, they declined until only small flocks continued to exist in the Midwest to its eastern boundary. Prairie Chickens prefer cover but scant cover when compared to that required by other gallinaceous or chicken-like birds such as the Quail, Partridge or Pheasant. We hunted Prairie Chickens many years ago in southern Illinois. The birds, in flocks of 10-20 or more, would feed through grain or stubble fields during the day, rest up at noon like Quail, feed again in the P.M., then fly to a field with knee-high cover to roost. If four hunters entered a feeding or roosting field from each of four directions, with or without a dog, the birds would lift or flush wild 100 yards ahead. Occasionally one person might get a shot or two. We observed them feeding in the Pheasant pens of Wisconsin friend a number of times. On each occasion they would approach from near the Illinois-Wisconsin state line at a height of 300 or 400 feet, rotating flying with long periods of coasting, circle a time or two and land near the large Pheasant pens and feed around the edge or in the middle of an adjacent wheat stubble field. When we observed them for long periods, it appeared that one or two birds were always "on guard" searching the area with heads up and highly alert. There were Prairie Chickens in central Illinois which we often flushed out of old orchards on abandoned farms. Such birds usually layed well for a point. The natives called them Pheasant, Partridge and occasionally Prairie Chicken.

We hope these fine birds continue to make a comeback in many states as they have in Missouri, where the Conservation Department is buying former prairie land and letting it grow up in the ancient prairie grasses and flora.

Several bird books report colonies of Prairie Chicken in many areas east of the Rocky Mountains. We hope the Conservation Department in such states will maintain a close watch and not schedule even a limited open season until the population of these great birds will stand it.

The Valley Quail and Sub-species, the California Quail

These colorful birds, with forward pointing head plume and buttons on top, populate the western coastal states from Washington south to southern California, nearly always in lands either part of or adjacent to the desert. They thrive in greater quantities than the other Western Desert Quail and spill over from California into similar habitat in Nevada and Arizona. They appear to like living near people who have large lawns and well watered semi-desert estates. We observed several large coveys on the campus at Stanford University and pairs of birds in residential areas of Palm Springs. They are fine eating birds which do not have a flavor of sage although they find something to eat on sagebrush. Their musical whistle is similar but not identical to that of the Bobwhite.

The Grey Partridge

The Grey Partridge, more commonly known as the Hungarian Partridge, arrived in the U.S. and Canada before the turn of the century, slightly before efforts were made to establish the Chukar on this continent. The "Hun" spread faster in most of the northern states adjacent to the Canadian border. They are sporty, one pound and reddish-grey in color, with red legs and reddish throat feathers. They are primarily grain and seed eaters which move in flocks twice the size of Bobwhite Quail, when moving from roost or rest areas to standing grain or stubble fields. We have hunted them in Wisconsin and Michigan and observed them on many occasions during the off-season feeding in snow covered corn fields in southern Wisconsin. They are difficult to approach when feeding in stubble fields, but so are other species of game birds. In cover, they hold fairly well for pointing breeds. They are more sporty to hunt with flushing dogs, which will dive head first into a flock and put the covey in flight with loud drumming of wings and a sharp "chick-chick." Fine eating birds, we hope they spread to more areas in more states.

The Chukar Partridge

The Chukar Partridge is a gaily colored foreigner which exists in some areas of the U.S., resulting from many efforts to adapt them to local climate and terrain and establish large breeding colonies. Our knowledge is limited to a few fairly large coveys of Chukars which we raised in Oregon while deer hunting. Our observation of the birds we flushed both walking and from horseback confirmed the reports of local hunters that they prefer rough foothill country and will run uphill and fly downhill when disturbed. We have shot a few in private and public hunting clubs when training dogs. Even in some areas they were strong flushers and, unlike Pheasant, failed to gain much altitude above ground. They have spread up and down the Pacific Coast but appeared to be more plentiful in Oregon than in adjoining states. There are small colonies of Chukars in a number of eastern states resulting from plantings by State Conservation Departments or birds released from private and public shooting clubs or bird dog field trials.

The Mountain Quail

The Mountain Quail have a single head feather that sticks up tall and straight like that worn by ancient tribes of American Indians. They prefer heavy brush cover near water like the Gambel's Quail. Their range includes the coastal states from Washington south to the Mexican border and Utah and areas of Arizona and New Mexico. We saw one or two coveys several times in foothills several miles south of Berkeley while working dogs with friends. One covey lifted 75 yards away when a planted common pigeon was shot during the training session. I marked the covey as it landed and walked-up several of the 15/20 bird covey. Ten minutes later a friendly game warden, who appeared on the scene to check on our activity since there was no open hunting season at the time, advised there were several coveys of Mountain Quail and California Quail in the general area.

The Harlequin Quail and the Scaled Quail

These two birds are residents of Mexico. The Scaled Quail has penetrated some of the border states like Arizona and New Mexico and is also found and hunted in West Texas where it is known as Blue Quail. Texans I know hunt them with Pointers, Retrievers and Springers, even though they are reluctant flushers. Both birds eat Mesquite, Acacia and other desert plants. We have never eaten either bird, but understand that Scaled Quail fattens up in West Texas on cultivated grain and stubble fields. The Harlequin Quail is also known as Fool's Quail, because of his extreme reluctance to flush or fly. Neither is a very exciting bird to hunt, which we learned in Mexico.

Gambel's Quail

Gambel's Quail resembles California Quail with its forward pointing head plume equipped with button on top. These birds are true desert Quail and prefer a desert habitat of mesquite and desert brush. Locally it is often referred to as Desert Quail. Their preference for desert habitat controls their range to California, north to Nevada and perhaps western Colorado. We hunted them a few times in Mexico, where they live in large quantity near the border and close to the mouth of the Colorado River. They can run like deer and do so when approached by man or dog. Pointing dogs apparently cannot always hold them even with quick, strong points.

Crested quail

TITLES FOR GUN DOG TRIAL WINNERS

The qualifications and standards for the several official titles awarded to gun dog winners and champions were established and are regulated by the American Field and the American Kennel Club. Both organizations also maintain separate stud book records and are the two largest recognized bodies which register purebred dogs. The mechanics of conducting competition and selecting winners are delegated by both organizations to certain local clubs which are required to file reports of trial results of each competitive event. The results are published in the official organ of the national organization which regulated the event: *The American Field* magazine and *Purebred Dogs—The American Kennel Gazette*. Qualifications for a title are slightly different for each organization.

The American Field limits its gun dog competition to field trials open for the most part to all pointing dog breeds. It delegates authority to a satellite organization The Amateur Field Trial Clubs of America, to regulate amateur field trial competition open to all pointing breeds.

The American Field prefix to designate an Open Champion is Champion, Open Derby Champion, Open Shooting Dog Champion and National Champion. The title may also designate an area such as Illinois Open Shooting Dog Champion or the species of game such as Grand National Grouse Champion or a specific breed such as National German Shorthaired Pointer Champion.